PARABLES FOR
THE PURPOSEFUL
WALK

PARABLES FOR THE PURPOSEFUL WALK

ARPress
ILLUMINATING IDEAS.
EMPOWERING VOICES

ARPress
45 Dan Road Suite 5
Canton, MA 02021

Hotline: 1(888) 821-0229
Fax: 1(508) 545-7580

Ordering Information:

Quantity sales. Special discounts are available on quantity purchases by corporations, associations, and others. For details, contact the publisher at the address above.

Printed in the United States of America.

ISBN-13:   Softcover   979-8-89389-416-5
              eBook   979-8-89389-415-8
              HardBack   979-8-89389-417-2

Library of Congress Control Number: 2024916988

CONTENTS

INTRODUCTION

BUT FIRST...

A WORD ABOUT THE PURPOSEFUL WALK

Every once in a while someone will ask how I came to call these writings of mine Parables. I always go back to the old Sunday School definition of a parable, which is "an earthly story with a heavenly meaning." Each of my Parables begins with a current event, or a personal experience, or sometimes just a thought that escaped from the back room of my mind. After a period of development each one ends with a spiritual or inspirational application. At least to my mind that meets the definition of a Parable. I hope you can agree.

The bulk of Parables in my first two books, "Parables for Plain People," and "More Parables for Plain People," were composed over a two year period. Since that time I have accumulated a large number of Parables that have been occasionally distributed as single inspirational pamphlets, used as material for inspirational talks and Bible studies, and other individual applications, but never until now gathered into another collection for a book.

Just as it was what I call a "Holy Nudge" that moved me to go into print with the first two groups, I received an urging that it was time to do the same with some of these more recent writings. The resulting collection is "Parables for the Purposeful Walk."

Many places in the Bible refer to our daily way of life in terms of walking. We are admonished to walk according to God's will for us, in the path that leads to His Kingdom. In this world of instant communication, information and mis-information, it is important for us to avoid the distractions that would cause us to hesitate, or run ahead, or stray from the Holy path.

My prayer for you is that you will find these writings to provide support and direction as you seek your own path, and, perhaps, to spiritually energize you as you follow purposefully—and with determination, strength and enthusiasm—God's path for you.

Please don't be distracted by the reference to events or facts that are no longer current. At the time of my referencing them, those things were for the most part the canvas upon which the Lord inspired me to compose words of instruction, caution, or encouragement...hopefully with a coating of humor to "help the medicine go down."

There is also a reference or two to the pet name "FooFoo the Wise," which one of my grandchildren gave to me. The "FooFoo" came from the familiar whistle with which I would occasionally call them. And once, after I answered a flood of questions from one he asked, "FooFoo, how did you get to be so wise?". Don't all parents and grandparents cherish the times when our admonitions are accepted as wisdom? I pray that you will discover the pearls of wisdom the Lord has hidden in these *Parables for the Purposeful Walk.*

"Hear this, all ye people;

give ear, all ye inhabitants of the world:

Both low and high, rich and poor, together;

My mouth shall speak of wisdom,

and the meditation of my heart shall be of understanding.

I will incline mine ear to a parable ... "

Psalm 49:1-4a (KJV)

PARABLE OF THE GOOD BOOK

I recently read an article which reminded me of a bumper sticker I saw in our church parking lot years ago. I believe it was part of a campaign by the American Bible Society to encourage daily Bible reading. The sticker sternly asked, "Read any Good Book lately?"

What do you think of when you hear the expression "Good Book"? In my mind, that doesn't refer to something on the New York Times Best Seller list...or to the Readers' Digest latest condensed book collection. It means THE Good Book...the Bible.

Now, I don't know about you and your background, but for myself...enrolled in the Sunday School Cradle Roll when I was six weeks old, taken or sent to Sunday School and church every Sunday we were in town, and Sunday School teacher on and off for forty years or so...when I think "Bible" I think King James Version.

Don't get me wrong. During a lifetime of Bible study and lesson preparation I have accumulated two dozen or more translations and paraphrases of the New Testament and the complete Bible. I have studied and read them all religiously (couldn't resist the pun) and found most of them helpful in understanding what God intended to communicate to us through His Word.

However, when it comes to power, eloquence and literary beauty, I always come back to the King James Version. Or, as one long-time Sunday School teacher in a small rural church told me, not entirely in jest, "Just give me the good old King James...just like God gave it to Moses!"

There is an increasing number of modern translations that are faithful to the original texts and made easier to read as literature. They are much more appealing to those that are new converts or merely new to the idea of Bible reading. They avoid the distractions of the stilted, old-fashioned speech and vocabulary of Elizabethan English. And, admittedly, anything that makes Bible reading easier and more attractive to ordinary people is good. Of course, that was the whole idea behind the preparation of a Bible written in a language of the people in the first place.

I still think that nothing quite carries the weight and effectiveness of "Ol' King Jimmy," as I heard one preacher call it, for public readings and memorization. Perhaps that's why it has stood the test of time.

In fact, that matter of standing the test of time is what generated the thought for this writing. For, you see, the year 2011 was the four hundredth anniversary of the introduction of the Authorized King James Version to the public.

A program aired on the local Public Broadcasting station related the story of the struggles to get the Scriptures into a language that not only the clergy but the common people could read and understand. The KJV was the culmination of that prolonged struggle.

I believe that there is one true indication of the value of having a translation of God's Word in a form that is easily accessible to everyone: The fact that the adversary has historically fought so strongly to prevent it...and, failing that, to discredit it and ridicule it.

As one radio preacher once said, "The devil doesn't bother you unless you're threatening his stuff." And nothing threatens his "stuff" like the harsh light of the Word of God. And the King James Version

of the Bible has beamed that light into the dark corners of the lowliest lives for four hundred years, and will continue to do so until that glorious day when the Lord returns.

Nonetheless, it is entirely as important that we continue to find and make available other faithful translations that will communicate the timeless truths of the Scriptures to those who are not charmed by what they may view as the stale and awkward cadences of the old translation.

Here's the point: Read some Good Book today, like your life depended on it...and it just might.

PARABLE OF THE BRIGHT CORNER

There was a very important time in my life when I spent ten years in Sunday School sitting in the floor with three-year olds. It started because when our youngest daughter was three, she was less than charmed with the idea of going into Miss Connie's Class.

Now Miss Connie was a real pro at working with the three's—after all, she had been teaching that class for thirty years or more—so it was no shock to her that one was a little bashful about coming into her class for the first time. Our Abigail was one of those rare cases that didn't yield to Miss Connie's calming strategies, however, so after a few weeks I was asked to consider coming in as her assistant teacher.

That did the trick. Abby settled down, I settled in....and after she "graduated" I stayed behind to love—and be loved on by—a ten-year parade of delightful (and sometimes extremely challenging) three-year-olds. They were truly in the tradition of the words of one of the songs they liked to sing, "Jesus Loves the Little Children," red and yellow, black and white...and, indeed, all precious in His—and my—sight.

We did a lot of singing in that class…mostly accompanied by me on my Autoharp. It was great to hear those little voices boisterously sing/shouting those simple songs Miss Connie had accumulated over the years. Songs like "L-O-V-E Love" and "Everybody happy say Amen."

One of Miss Connie's favorites, although a little too complicated for the children, was "Brighten the Corner Where You Are," with words that encouraged them not to wait for some special occasion to begin serving Jesus, but to begin right away, wherever you are. Connie related that as a small child she thought the words were "Right on the corner where you are." Either way, I think the meaning is pretty much the same.

I have thought about Miss Connie…and the singing children… and the Bright/Right Corner…many times over the years. I think about them as I observe the news reports of how individuals— often whole communities—respond to the natural disasters that sometimes engulf them.

Some are grateful, some critical, some miserable. Some people do fall into misfortune and ruin. Most take their circumstances with them, for better or worse, to the corner where they land.

I have thought about the Bright Corner this Spring, as I watched the blossoms and leaves suddenly bursting open in brilliant displays of color. Each year seems to have its outstanding performers. Sometimes it's the dogwoods, sometimes the azaleas, or the flowering quince.

When it comes to Bright Corners, however, my award this year goes to one dogwood sapling in our neighborhood. Although this is not their best year, the dogwoods are glorious, just the same …the whites are gleaming and the pinks ranging from a shy, blushing pink to an almost scarlet hue. Not all dogwoods are created equal, however, and this one young sapling was especially notable because of its lack of blossoms. In fact, its entire effort was invested in a single flower, tentatively extended on the end of a long and otherwise bare twig of a branch.

At first I thought, "How pitiful! How sad, among all the beautiful, showy abundance of the surrounding mature trees to have only one puny blossom to show for a season's production." Then I remembered the principle of The Bright Corner. To paraphrase my dad's words, the

Lord isn't going to hold that dogwood responsible for what any of the other dogwoods do...only for how faithfully it used the resources with which it was blessed and brightened its own corner.

The only way to live a joyful, liberated life is to bloom where we're planted...brighten the corner where we are...and the only way to do that is to be in tune with the Lord's plan for our lives. So, in Miss Connie's words, "Brighten the corner...right on the corner...where you are." Besides, when you share the blessing with which you've been blessed, you get to enjoy it twice.

PARABLE OF THE FLYING TRAPEZE

I don't know about you, but I've always loved the circus. No matter that I haven't been to one in ten years or so, since the time I took several of my grandchildren to a small, one-ring, one-elephant circus at the local fairground. And that was the first time since I took their mother and aunts, many years before, to see the famous Ringling Brothers-Barnum and Bailey Circus at the Omni Arena in Atlanta. But I still love the circus.

I remember when I was a small boy and Dad drove us by the place where the Ringling Brothers Circus had set up the old-fashioned big-top, with the gypsy camp of roust-abouts and performers pitched around it, in the outskirts of Atlanta. There were elephants, camels, zebras and Percheron stallions seen processing along the street, on their way to or from performances or to perform some of the necessary labor associated with setting up and maintaining the circus "camp".

Unfortunately, the romantic era of the large circus operating under the "big top" circus tent, came to an end shortly after the July 6, 1944, disaster when that same Ringling Brothers tent burned in Hartford, Connecticut, with over 165 fatalities. But disasters such as that were foreign to small boys, and recalling the excitement and drama of sitting in the grandstands inside a big tent and watching the exotic pageantry unfold still holds the imagination captive.

Nowadays, circuses like the RB-B&B hold forth in large auditoriums, convention centers and arenas; but the magic can still be felt when the band begins to play...the animals, clowns and performers parade in their outlandishly gaudy, brightly colored costumes, waving grandly to the audience as they troop around the floor.

The first time I actually remember attending a circus was when Mom took me to see the Shrine Circus at the old Atlanta Municipal Auditorium. That was about the largest indoor venue in town in those days, and in addition to events like the curcus it was home to symphony orchestras, international ballet performances, operas...both grand and "Grand Ole" style...all night gospel sings, rock concerts, wrestling matches and the annual Ice-Capades. Not to mention the occasional convention. Today I suppose we would call it truly a multi-use facility. In those days it was known among many who performed there simply as "the barn."

That Shrine Circus was my first exposure to the drama of all the aerial acts. There were the performers on the high wire, walking, dancing, juggling and cycling their way across the auditorium, breathtakingly high over the awed audience. There was the apparently drunken clown, stumbling his way up the rope-ladder, and as the horrified on-lookers watched, inching and lurching his unsteady way out onto the wire...only to rip off the clown costume, revealing one of the talented wire-walkers. Ta-dah! What a relief!

I think, however, that my favorite acts at the circus...even over the clowns, the big cat trainers and the horse and dog acts...were the trapeze troupes. The trim, muscular men in their tights...the beautiful women in their sequined leotards, covered in precious jewels...their agile yet majestic ascent up the ladder to the tiny platform...somehow packed the maximum amount of drama into their all-too-brief performance.

The first to take the air was always the Catcher, sturdily built with a wide wrist band on each arm to assist in providing a firm grip to his comrades. Next in a continuous succession came the Flyers...other men and women with their gravity-defying feats, swinging, balancing and dangling from the trapezes as they soared back and forth. The usual finale was a series of nerve-racking single, double and, perhaps, triple somersaults into the dependable hands of the catcher.

I've seen many trapeze acts since that first trip to the Shrine Circus, including a show that ran for many years on Saturday morning television, called "The Sealtest Big Top," but the thrill is always the same. And each time I see one of those performances the same thoughts come to mind.

Those glamorous "flyers" are always the ones to draw the applause and admiration of the audience. However, their exciting airborne gymnastics would be impossible without the dependable performance of the catcher.

The catcher is the first to rise above the arena floor, and the last to descend. His skill, strength and timing are the factors that make the difference between a successful performance and a disaster. In spite of his key role, he almost always defers to his aerobatic companions when the time comes for the bows to the appreciative audience.

From time to time, we each face circumstances where we have come to the end of our resources...when we are threatened beyond our capacity to cope. At those times, we can either throw up our hands in despair, or we can trust ourselves to the hands of the divine Catcher, who alone is both capable and trustworthy to safely bring us through every disaster.

From my own personal experience, I can assure you...if you want more than anything else to do what the Lord wants you to...that He is there, ready and able to receive you and bring you through even the worst trial.

I can also promise you that if the Lord is your Catcher there's no need for a safety net. He never misses, no matter how much we may feel like we're going to fall. Just check out Jude 24 and 25, if you don't believe me (the emphasis is mine):

"Now unto him that is able to *keep you from falling*, and to present you faultless before the presence of his glory with exceeding joy, To the only wise God, our Savior, be glory and majesty, dominion and power, both now and forever. Amen." And Amen!

PARABLE OF THE INHERITANCE

I recently went shopping for birthday presents for one of the granddaughters and a great-grandson. I hadn't thought about it before, but it suddenly struck me how differently one shops for the "grands" and the "greats" than for one's own children.

Every parent knows what I mean, I'm sure. With your children there's a constant conflict between buying something practical versus something frivolous. There's always a balancing act between those two choices, isn't there? Especially when money and price are important.

I remember as a young married person...a husband at that...that my first consideration in choosing a gift for my dear wife was "Now, let's see...what does she need? What can she use?" And for far too many years those were the types of gifts she received from her loving spouse.

Eventually, though, her stoic acceptance of those carefully selected offerings reached its limits. She finally confided...in a most loving, but firm way...that the gift she *really* enjoyed most was something frivolous. And I later learned that ruled out anything with a cord attached. (I must add, in fairness, that in our more mature years she admitted that she had come to appreciate those practical gifts a lot more than she used to.)

In thirty-five or so years of teaching Sunday School, and quite a few spent training others in personal evangelism and how to share their Christian witness, I have done a lot of studying and thinking about the nature of gifts. In order to understand what a gift is, though, one must first learn what a gift is not.

Almost all men...and in recent years many women as well...get up each morning, dress, eat breakfast and go to work. That work provides their livelihood in the form of wages. Those wages are determined by the type and amount of work done, and its value to an employer. The more work, the more pay. The more important the work, and the better its performance, the greater the amount of the reward. It's as simple as that.

Gifts, however, are a lot more complex than that. Roget's Thesaurus lists over one hundred synonyms for the noun form of the word "gift," nearly twice as many as it shows for the noun form of "wages." Whether called an award...or a bequest, donation, endowment, grant, inheritance, largess, legacy, talent, tip or treat...a gift, simply speaking, is something of value voluntarily transferred by one person to another without compensation. And, in its purest form, without condition.

So... wages are the expected reward for tasks that have been satisfactorily performed by one party on behalf of another. They must be earned by performance or behavior. A gift, on the other hand, *cannot* be earned and has little or no relationship to performance or behavior. And even when there is such a relationship, it is minimal in comparison to the value of the gift. Otherwise, it becomes wages, right?

The nature of gifts and wages came into focus for me recently through a couple of experiences. I recently adopted a "mostly" Black Labrador Retriever named Suzy Q. When I give the commands "Sit! Stay!" she obeys—at least, most of the time. After she has remained for the required amount of time, I give her what trainers call a "treat." But it's not really, is it? It's wages...paid for correct behavior. When we are sitting quietly (that doesn't happen often with an active puppy) and I give her a goody for no reason, *that's* a treat...a gift, just because I love her.

Secondly, I was reminded that when one receives an inheritance from a loved one who has graduated into the Kingdom, it is based upon a relationship, not effort, performance or the quality or length of service. The feature of an inheritance that distinguishes it from other gifts is that in order to receive it someone must die.

As a believer, I can never think about wages and gifts...or inheritances...without calling to mind Ephesians 2: 8 and 9, where Paul writes, "For by grace are ye saved through faith; and that not of yourselves, it is the gift of God—not of works, lest any man should boast." And in Romans 6:23 he wrote, "For the wages of sin is death, but the gift of God is eternal life through Jesus Christ our Lord."

Here it is in a nutshell: by the simple act of faith in the claims of Jesus we can inherit the unearned, extravagant gift of eternal life. No act of goodness...nor works of the sincerest devotion...are of sufficient value in God's eyes to earn the blessing of eternal life with Him. Only a personal relationship with the One Who died in payment of the penalty for our sin is sufficient to assure we can receive that precious inheritance.

Gives a whole new meaning to the phrase "Being in the Will," doesn't it?

Are you? In His Will, I mean. I pray that you are.

PARABLE OF THE SILENT SAINT

A fter having a hot, dry Summer, we've come crashing up against the Winter Solstice with the first really cold weather...coldest since last February, one reporter reported. In fact, one weather "dudette" said we recently experienced the coldest daytime temperature in forty-three years. Or was it thirty-four? I forget. Anyway, it's been very cold.

Yesterday, as Suzy Q and I were foraging and migrating dutifully around the neighborhood, there was an almost-visible misting of snow on the ground...and, before we arrived back at our starting point there began to appear a slight, one-flake-at-a-time misting of snow. It was just enough to hint at the possibility...but not quite enough to threaten boastfully...of a *real* snowfall.

Even an occasional reader of these parables can guess how my imagination took the leap from that ever-so-slight possibility to recollections of bygone snow events...and, if that is your guess, you would be correct. My mental recorder began flashing scenes from the first snow I experienced as a three-year-old and rapidly fast-forwarded to the Sunday morning it had snowed enough in Atlanta that church services at Second-Ponce de Leon Baptist Church were canceled.

That particular Sunday snow storm stuck in my mind mainly because of one thing. The cancellation of the services had been widely announced on both radio and TV, but, just in case, the pastor, Dr.

Russell Dilday, had gotten someone with 4-wheel drive to take him to the church to notify any hardy soul who had ventured out that there would be nothing going on there.

It was a good thing he did, too, because two people did eventually arrive—only the Lord knows how. Mrs. Sexta Strickland had prevailed on her daughter to drive her to church, as she had for many, many, many years.

Ms. Sexta was one of those special people. If they still gave Sunday School Perfect Attendance pins, she would have had to walk bent almost double, dragging her chain of pins like Marley's ghost. You see, she was well into her nineties, still faithfully teaching her Sunday School class...and if she had ever missed a Sunday, there was no one old enough to remember...records simply didn't go back that far. And she wasn't going to let one of Atlanta's worst blizzards in decades break her record. Nosiree.

I remember Ms. Sexta well, because for several years she had my dad print an annual booklet of her collected writings which she would give to family, friends and selected individuals. As a Sunday School teacher, she had accumulated many kinds of articles and observations, numerous original poems and not a few autobiographical sketches. It was my job to get them ready for printing, and I found them to be fascinating.

She was the closest I will ever come, I suppose, to knowing a genuine pioneer. She told of many adventures and experiences, most of which I've forgotten. However, there's one tale of her exploits that I do recall, and that has to do with the fact that, among other skills she possessed, she was one of very few female telegraph operators. Like in the old western movies, where you see the operator at the train depot, rapidly working the key, tapping out a message in Morse Code. That's Ms. Sexta.

As striking and special as she was, though, it wasn't the fact that she came to church through a raging snow storm that impresses me so much. You see, at almost 100 years old, Ms. Sexta hadn't driven in years. As determined...and, yes, as stubborn...as she was, she would have never been able to pile up such an impressive record on her own.

On the Sunday after the storm, the congregation recognized her for her dogged faithfulness in coming to church. And they certainly should have.

As we were leaving the Sanctuary, however, my dad stopped her daughter (I think that it's noteworthy that I'm not sure of her name... she lived in Ms. Sexta's shadow a lot...but I think it was Ms. Corbett) and told her, "I just wanted you to know that I realize that the only way your mom has been able to get here so faithfully, even through the snow, was that you were available to drive her."

Her response was quite characteristic. She said, "You know, you're the first one to ever mention that. Thank you."

Don't take anything away from the example of Ms. Sexta. She was, indeed, remarkable. But for every Sexta Strickland, there must be many Silent Saints, faithfully performing unremarkable duties without ever seeking...and, usually without receiving...acknowledgement of their contributions.

So, don't be disappointed or discouraged if your contributions to the on-going of the Kingdom go unnoticed by those around you. The Lord keeps track of such things and has a special reward for His Silent Saints. And, I promise, it's worth the wait.

PARABLE OF THE GRAND PLAN

"Gloom, despair and agony on me-e!
Deep dark depression, excessive misery-y!
If it weren't for bad luck, I'd have no luck at all!
Gloom, despair and agony on me-e-e!"

It's hard to believe that it was so long ago that the TV show "Hee-Haw" was popular. It ran from 1969 to 1971, and then in syndication for another twenty years or so. I'm not so sure that it can't still be seen on cable somewhere.

Any fan of the show will remember the lyrics quoted above as one of the recurring themes on the show. And whether you're a fan or not you can hear those familiar lines sung or recited from time to time even in these days.

As a matter of fact, they come to mind quite often as I watch or listen to the current day's news reports. It seems as if the only events that reporters and commentators find newsworthy are those that reflect "gloom, despair and agony...deep, dark depression, excessive misery... bad luck." Besides that, they have eliminated the original humor and added in its place desperation and terror.

In view of these realities, there's little wonder that many who have no experience of a personal relationship with a Creator/God can question how a loving God could allow these disasters and this misfortune to plague so many innocent people. Even the faithful sometimes have doubts.

Years ago, as a young Sunday School teacher, I was eager to find commentaries and illustrations to make the lessons more interesting and helpful. That was when I came across an article in which the writer attempted to explain the presence of sin and evil in a world that God had pronounced "Good."

In what was, perhaps, a variation of the Old Testament story of Job, he talked of a discussion between God and the one the Bible names Satan, who is described as the wisest, most beautiful and powerful of the angels. The adversary, who considered himself God's equal, argued, "Of course, your creatures will be obedient. They have no choice. They are, after all your creatures."

In this writer's imaginary confrontation, God proposed a plan that would prove the adversary was not as wise and powerful as he believed himself to be...and certainly not a match for Himself.

As I recall it, the plan was something like this: God would create a sort of laboratory, an environment limited by physical space and time. In that laboratory he would place a species of creature with a living soul, made in His spiritual image, just as the adversary had been. He would place in that lab all the things these creatures would need to survive and prosper. Then He would call these creatures Mankind. Because they were created in His image, Mankind would possess a quality that the other creatures in the lab would not have...freedom of will, whereby they could choose whether they would obey His commands or not.

Next, God allowed the adversary to enter this laboratory and do his best to prove that he could do anything God could do...even better. Finally, God decreed that at the end of the experiment they would meet for a final evaluation of the results of the contest.

The ground rules were fairly simple. God would remain all-powerful, all-knowing, all-wise and able to occupy all of space and time simultaneously. He could make His presence known to any and all of Mankind through visual, spoken or mental communication. The only power He would surrender was the power to *make* Mankind love, obey and follow Him.

The adversary, on the other hand, was free to use any power, tactic and skill he could muster to try to win the loyalty of Mankind. In spite of his wisdom and cunning, however, he had limitations. He couldn't be in all places and all times at once, even though he could, like a general of a vast army, impart elements of his knowledge and strength to his minions, his imps and demons assigned to each person throughout time and space.

All of the adversary's tactics and methods were designed to break the spiritual bond between God and Mankind and to win as many of them to himself as possible. That's where the "gloom, despair and agony" come in.

Those who have never developed a consciousness of One Who provides for, and watches over, those who are faithful to Him can be easily led to question how a loving God could allow these miseries to befall His creatures. They are hapless victims to the wiles of the adversary.

When the experiment is over, however, when the Grand Plan is completely worked out, and all the persuasive arguments, proofs, theories and excuses are presented before the throne of the Judge of all things, the adversary will be forced to acknowledge the supremacy of Almighty God. The adversary and all who believed his cunning lies will go to a place of eternal punishment. All those who proved faithful to God will participate in the glories of His everlasting Kingdom.

So...when your days resonate with the songs of gloom, despair and agony played in your ear by the adversary's minions, remember the songs of joy, victory and "Sunshine In My Soul" available to all who put their trust in Jesus...all those "Marching to Zion." That's God's Grand Plan.

PARABLE OF THE SHADY TRAIL

Recently my wife Joyce and I took one of our regular trips to visit her family in Tennessee. On this occasion we stayed with our dear friends, the Powells, who operate a delightful retreat on their family farm in Walland, which is located on what is called in brochures as "the quiet side of the Smokies."

The Powell Farm is one of those places where if you really must "do" something you have to go somewhere else. Don't misunderstand me. There is plenty to do just a short drive away: The Smoky Mountains National Park, Pigeon Forge, Dollywood, Gatlinburg, Tuckaleechee Caverns, and so forth. However, if your idea of a retreat is sitting quietly, reading, relaxing, and enjoying the stirring vistas of the rolling mountains in a peaceful pastoral setting, then the Powell Farm is just the place.

While we were there, we took advantage of a little spare time and decided to take a stroll down the gravel road that leads through the property. The late afternoon had cooled off a bit and the sights and sounds were beckoning.

As we walked, we talked softly so as not to disturb the peace. We talked of our joy at being able to take hiking trails in the mountains, listening to the sounds in the silence of a drowsy summer afternoon;

enjoying the occasional bursts of color from the season's final wildflower exhibition, and watching the bees and butterflies as they do their flower-hopping before the blossoms fade away.

Aside from our quiet conversation, the persistent scrunch of our tread on the gravel was the only sound to invade the peace and solitude. Even that was barely enough to disturb the small family of wild turkeys and the occasional horse grazing drowsily in the pasture as we passed.

We walked on easily, unbothered by the uneven gravel surface, the slight ruts made by a passing farm vehicle, and once in a while a rebellious tree root that ventured to cross the road, perhaps, just to get to the other side. The grade was easy and perfectly suited to our pace.

My Joyce and I basked in the brilliant warmth of the road's sunlit stretches. However, it seemed that just when the sun's caresses became too oppressive, we would enter a place where the over-arching trees provided welcoming shade to cool our bodies and soothe our spirits.

I noticed something interesting about those cool, shady parts of the road, though. In some places the shade was just a little too dark, almost gloomy, the cool just slightly less friendly, perhaps, at least in my imagination, a little bit threatening. The ruts, rocks, and roots were harder to notice, becoming obstacles capable of causing trips and stumbles.

As we paced through one of those too-cool-to-be-comfortable places we came to a slight curve in the road. As we rounded the turn we saw ahead, as if we were emerging from a tunnel, the bright, welcoming sunlit pasture before us. With that encouragement we ventured on until we reached the comfort of the Powell's back porch. The spectacular scenery, the silence, and the solitude were well worth the expense of energy.

As I relaxed in the fan-stirred breeze of the porch, I thought about our walk down that road, and how similar it is to our travel down Life's Road. Sometimes Life's Road is level, smooth and sunlit. That's when we find life challenging and go about achieving satisfying results.

At other times we find the shade to be welcoming and comforting, offering relaxation, renewal and recovery. Life's shady lanes are altogether as important to our well-being as the bright highways of Life's accomplishments.

However, you and I have each traveled parts of Life's Road which were neither exciting and encouraging, nor welcoming and nurturing. Sometimes Life's Road is dark and threatening, and travel is difficult and distressing. Sometimes the gloom and despair are overwhelming, the pain of travel is too much to bear.

When you find yourself on this road you can go to MapQuest or Google Maps all you want, but you'll not be able to find a suitable alternate route. Your only way out is to follow it to its conclusion, when you will eventually emerge into the light. That's Life.

As I go walking down Life's Road each day, whether it's sunlit, shady or dark and threatening, I like to think of the story of Adam in the garden of Eden. He walked the same kind of road without a care. Why? Because God created him to walk with Himself.

The Psalmist wrote about walking through the valley of the shadow, without fear, because he knew that the Shepherd was walking with him. You and I have been given that same assurance.

So, enjoy the trip. And when you hit those shadowy stretches just remember that if you keep in step with the Shepherd, and keep on pushing, you'll get past the shady trails of Life and emerge into the glorious sunlight.

Finally, remember this: the road you're traveling is not a dead end like the one Joyce and I followed. If you keep on walking with the Shepherd, you'll experience the glorious ending that He has in store for you. You don't need to rush, either, because it'll be there waiting for you when you arrive in your time, if you just keep going.

PARABLE OF THE HUMMINGBIRD WARS

Our house has a stone terrace across the front with lovely plants and shrubbery around the edges, thanks to the previous owners. With a glass-topped table and wrought-iron patio chairs, it makes a very pleasant place to sit and relax, perhaps with a cup of coffee and a book.

Our breakfast table overlooks the terrace and we enjoy the view as we sit at mealtimes. My Joyce has placed a birdbath and several bird feeders about the area so we can watch the amazing variety of birds that come to feed and bathe almost year-around.

Another element she added, which has brought us many moments of fascination and joy, is a pair of hummingbird feeders. One of them she can see out the window as she works at the kitchen sink, and the other is just outside the window by the breakfast table. I've never seen so many of the tiny creatures from such close range.

It is mesmerizing to observe these little guys, about the size of my thumb, as they sometimes perch and sometimes hover, suspended in mid-air on almost invisible wings, and with perfect accuracy place a needle-like proboscis repeatedly into the heart of that plastic blossom.

When I'm outside at the patio table, and one of these feathered wonders visits the feeders there is the almost imperceptible sound of those beating wings that reminds me of Luke Skywalker from Star Wars, readying his light saber to do battle. I don't know if that has occurred to anyone else, but that's what it makes me think of.

There is one aspect of this creature's habits, however, that I find a little upsetting. Like so many creatures in their natural habitats, the hummingbird is extremely territorial. It seems incapable of enjoying its existence when another of its species is in sight.

In my experience, no matter how many well-stocked feeders are in the vicinity, no matter how long a hummingbird has spent drinking its fill, it will still streak off to attack any fellow of its kind impertinent enough to invade its territory. Among these wee warriors there seems to be no concept of selfless sharing or generosity. This is survival of the fittest carried to extreme limits.

Now, of course, we're accustomed to seeing this behavior among predators of all sizes and species. And when resources are limited, competition for food and territory is considered natural. It just seems so unnecessary, though, when there is plenty of food and space to accommodate all.

As puzzling and thought-provoking as this trait is among the hummingbird community, it is much more disturbing to realize that it also occurs much higher in the food chain, among the human race. What is acceptable among carnivores, and, yes, even among harmless hummingbirds, is abhorrent among mankind.

Hardly a news day goes by that we fail to see reports of bullies, cheats, thieves and murderers attacking and taking things from others. Driving them away from their homes and property. Why? Not because they are without the necessities of life, but because they merely want *more*.

So many of our fellow humans are like the seagulls in the movie *Finding Nemo*, who, when they spot a fish on the pier, all rush forward crying, "Mine!" "Mine!" "Mine!" Human nature seems to program us to think, "First come, first served," and that the biggest and meanest gets the most.

As you go about your daily routine today, are you going to fight the hummingbird wars, insisting upon having your way and serving yourself, no matter at whose expense? Or are you going to be thoughtful of others, patient, helpful, loving, and generous with your resources?

As Believers we have been given the gift of eternal life through Jesus Christ. It is our mission to share what we have earned and what we have been given, as a means of attracting others into the Kingdom of Heaven when we each are called in our time. After all, there's plenty for each of us.

PARABLE OF THE SCARY PUMPKIN

I t's that time of year again. The mornings are getting cooler, the Encore Azaleas are into their last encore, and the leaves are beginning to turn, and then turn loose.

All the stores have Halloween candy and costumes on full display. One store we visited the other day was so afraid of missing a sales opportunity that they had skeletons, turkeys and Santa Claus decorations side by side on the shelf. And of course, there are plenty of pumpkins around.

As interesting and tempting as all this seasonal emphasis is, that's not what I wanted to write about this morning. In fact, this sequence of events could have happened at any time of year.

Since my Joyce and I moved our home into our current house, we have been aware of several cats that roam the neighborhood freely. They don't wear any sort of collar, and seem to come and go at will, so we assume they haven't chosen a permanent residence.

One of them is quite friendly. She is almost completely black with a small white bib and white anklets on all four feet. She will walk up to anyone, meow profusely, and make it clear that a kind word, neighborly pat and generous "skritch" behind the ears would be welcome and appreciated. We have been known to offer all the above, in addition to an occasional cup of milk.

The second one is quite skittish, wary of the approach of any person. This one, also a female, is a light orange, almost blond color and usually appears just a little disheveled. We aren't privileged to a close inspection of this one, but we suspect that she is an older cat and has perhaps been mistreated. We've never heard her make any sort of sound.

This second cat will sit on our front walk two times a day, like a bird in the wilderness, waiting to be fed. However, at the first slight sound of the front door lock she begins to shy away. When the door is opened, she quickly slinks into the nearby shrubbery, where she will furtively watch to see if we have anything in store for her. Only when we are out of sight, and the door is safely latched will she cautiously emerge to survey the scene. She usually finds a cup of cat food and some milk.

A few weeks ago, we had the pleasure of keeping our great-grandson Kaleb for a week. During that time both the cats came around at regular times and he asked what their names were. When we told him we didn't know if they had names, he was sad and proceeded to give each one a suitable name. For some reason known only to Kaleb, the black cat was called Katrina. For a more obvious reason the orange one was dubbed Pumpkin. And, thus, at least in our family's conversation, they became.

If animals were allowed in the house, I'm sure that Katrina would readily visit and could be coaxed to become a lap cat. However, to my knowledge Pumpkin has never allowed anyone, other cats included, within a six-to-eight-foot radius. When that boundary is challenged, she quickly withdraws a safe distance to observe what may happen.

As you might suspect, since we began to set out cat food and milk in the morning and evening, Pumpkin arrives on the front walk to receive her daily blessing. After dining she will often stretch out on the patio for a brief, restless nap before retiring to her safe place. Wherever that is.

Although she is ready and willing to receive the food and drink, we offer, she is afraid to take the chance that we might be kind to her in other ways. What a sad way to live out an existence.

As I observe the events in the world around me, it occurs to me that there are multitudes of people out there just like our scary Pumpkin. They are quick to say prayers to whatever Power they recognize...prayers for blessing, help in times of difficulty, healing in times of sickness, feeding in times of hunger, deliverance in times of danger.

At the same time, they are reluctant to put themselves into the hands of that Power, to be engaged in faithful service. At the first sign of an approach by that Power, they shy away and withdraw, choosing to enjoy the benefits without any obligation to service.

I have had Jesus in my heart for many years now, and I have assurance that the Power above all powers is Almighty God. Although He has no reason to show me favor, He blesses me anyway. For the first years after becoming a Believer, I was a little like Pumpkin, keeping Him just out of reach, lest He draw me into something that I didn't like. I would show up regularly to receive His blessing, then return to my own comfort zone until the next feeding time. I'm so glad that changed.

If only our scary Pumpkin would trust us, we could love her and pet her, and make her feel at home in our presence. The Lord has that same desire for us. He wants us to love Him and trust Him to guide and protect us, to keep us safe and deliver us as we go through sorrows and dangers.

Don't go through your life as a scary Pumpkin. "Trust in the Lord with all your heart, and lean not on your own understanding; In all your ways acknowledge Him, And He shall direct your paths." (Proverbs 3:5-6, NKJV)

PARABLE OF THE SOUL SONG

Have you ever had one of those times when a song somehow got loose inside your head and seemed to get into everything, and you couldn't get it to go away? That happens to me all the time...so often, in fact, that I hardly even try to get rid of it anymore. If songs were cats, my brain would be like the house of that dear soul I heard about that couldn't resist taking in every wandering feline that came to the door looking for a hand-out.

Now that I think about it, that's probably not a bad analogy. If you've ever had a cat around the house, you know what I mean. They wander through the place at will...come and go as they please... demand attention, no matter what else you have in mind...curl up in your lap—or in the middle of whatever you're working on—and insist on being scratched behind the ears. Some days a song can be just like that, can't it?

When I go for a necessary stroll with my canine girlfriend Suzy Q, I often find myself humming...whether out loud or in my mental conservatory...pacing along to whatever tune was on the TV or radio as we walked out the door. Sometimes the tune is suggested by something that has been said, or that I have read. No matter the source of the inspiration, that tune will continue to nuzzle me and require scratching until I can coax it to leave me in peace.

Since I was asked to write a brief article about my experiences as a member of Cobb Festival Singers, my mental lap has been invaded by such a tune and the words that so clearly express my feelings. The music and the lyrics were composed by Robert Lowry in 1860, possibly based upon an old Quaker hymn. Let me share the first verse with you:

My life flows on in endless song, Above earth's lamentation.

I hear the sweet though far-off hymn that hails a new creation.

Through all the tumult and the strife, I hear the music ringing.

It finds an echo in my soul—How can I keep from singing?

It has always been so, from the most primitive tribe to the most sophisticated civilization, that the heights and depths of emotion most often find their expression in music. From exuberant songs of joy when things go well, to the melancholy minor key in times of difficulty, sadness and woe, music can be the safety valve that keeps our joys and sorrows from overwhelming us.

How can I keep from singing, indeed! Just ask my daughters, or anyone else who knows me. I will sing at the drop of a hat. Shoot! You don't even have to drop it...just touch the brim and I'll sing. Just give me a nod...a wink...anything. I can't *not* sing. I even sang a few lines from a favorite hymn to our waitress in a restaurant the other night.

There's a line from an old spiritual that goes, "My soul's so happy that I can't sit down." In my case I can say that "my soul's so full that I can't stop singing." Whatever my circumstances, there always seems to be a song in my heart that suits the situation.

Where do the soul's songs come from? How is it that there's always just the right one handy whatever the occasion? My grandchildren would suggest, perhaps, that they were downloaded by the spiritual equivalent of iTunes into my mental MP3 player and stored on my infinite hard-drive.

There is a much simpler explanation. As I told that waitress, when one has Jesus in the heart there is a fullness that can't help but overflow to each person with whom we come in contact. It may be in the form of words or music...or it could be in the form of actions, without need for words or music. If the Lord is in control of your life there's no way you can keep the soul's songs to yourself.

PARABLE OF THE FINEST WINE

Johnny Hart was widely known as the thoughtful and creative Christian cartoonist of the comic strip BC. He has long been one of my favorite commentators on human nature and the human condition, and was masterful at finding the humor in life situations.

I have kept a copy of one of my favorite BC strips for many years. In the first frame we find the main character, BC, earnestly praying, "God, if you're up there, give me a sign." The next frame shows a tremendous, earthshaking CRASH. In the final frame we see imbedded in the ground in front of BC a large, theater marquee bearing the message "I'M UP HERE!"

Have you ever thought how great it would be if only God would always make His presence and His will for us as plain and easy to recognize as that? I know I have.

Although occasionally we read about the burning bushes and blinding lights from heaven, most of the time the Lord reveals Himself to us in much more subtle...and one might say, even polite... ways, through whispers and gentle nudges. As we go stumbling and bumbling through our daily lives, we so easily overlook...or ignore... His signs and quiet coaxing. And so often miss the joy of finding and following His Will.

Sometimes the Lord invests His revelations in familiar everyday events where we can miss the signs of His presence and participation if we're not careful. It is easy to see them as "Wow!" moments without acknowledging His hand at work.

For example, In his account of Jesus at the wedding in Cana of Galilee, John tells us of the first public sign, or miracle, of His brief ministry. You know the story well, I'm sure.

Jesus and His disciples were attending the wedding of what was most likely close family friends. Such weddings lasted several days, and by custom were more or less public events in the villages of that day.

The wedding planner mentioned to Mary, mother of Jesus, that the celebration had been such a success that they had almost run out of wine. That could have been a disaster, and a blow to the reputation of the wedding party's family, if a remedy wasn't found fast.

Mary wasted no time in "suggesting," as only a mother who understands her child could, that Jesus could solve the problem. Even though the Lord hadn't intended to start His ministry that week, He was obedient to His mother's urging to "do something," and instructed the servants to fill the water jars, reserved for the ritual cleansing ceremonies constantly observed during the feast, and take samples to the manager of the event.

You could give yourself a headache trying to decide whether the water was immediately turned into wine when it was poured into the jars...or became wine as it was dipped into the serving pitchers... or when it was poured into the individual goblets...or even remained water until the instant it was sipped. But don't bother yourself about that.

The fact is simply that the planner, who probably knew good wine when he tasted it, said something like, "Wow! This is *really* good wine. Most folks would have put out the 'good stuff' to begin with and, when everyone was too wasted to notice, bring out the Wal-Mart Wine-in-a-box to save money." Or words to that effect.

Unbelievers and critics, looking for a "Gotcha!" moment to use against Christians, have gleefully pointed to this event as proof that drinking is OK, since it was condoned...even made possible...by Jesus. As usual, they miss the point of the story. And it isn't even about the kind, or quality of the wine...or the amount consumed...or the nature of the event where it was served.

In fact, I don't even think it's about the wine at all.

I believe that what John is demonstrating for us is the simple fact that whenever we involve the Lord in our plans, and trust Him to help us in times of difficulty and stress, He always comes through with the finest wine imaginable. He takes what we have available...the simple materials and acts designated for ritualistic observance...and turns them into the highest quality sacrifice, fit for offering to His Father.

Moreover, He is always willing and able to provide that finest wine in overflowing abundance when we trust Him to do so. As He promised, "I am come that they might have life, and that they might have it more abundantly." (John 10:10b)

Life filled with the finest wine. All you can drink. May I offer you some? It's already paid for.

PARABLE OF THE PEPPERMINT PIG

With all the "gloom and doom" articles in the news media these days, it's a relief to come across one every once in a while, that contains no dire warnings, no shocking revelations, no thinly veiled attempts to sway one's opinion...just a bit of trivia that can provide a brief "think break." I found just such an article today and thought I'd share it.

While paging through the serious, distressing and troublesome news items on the day's internet offering, my eye was caught by a headline that was just whimsical enough to make me stop and pull up the story. It read "Peppermint Pigs a Smashing Tradition in NY." Now, how could one not be intrigued by that?

According to the AP news reporter, a company in Saratoga Springs, New York, markets a line of peppermint candy molded in the form of a pig, each one of which is wrapped with a small silver hammer. The pigs come in three sizes, the largest of which weighs a full pound.

It seems that the idea is based upon an old European tradition and evolved from the marzipan pigs made by European candymakers as good luck symbols. One theory about the change into its current form is that candymakers in Saratoga Springs resort hotels changed to peppermint hard candy because it was easier to make than marzipan.

Whatever the origin, the tradition calls for the pig to be passed around the dinner table and smashed with the hammer to bring good luck to the family. And, whether or not smashing peppermint pigs brings good luck to anyone else, it has indeed brought good fortune to one New York confectioner.

I'm not sure why, but something about that little story appeals to me. Perhaps it's because I like peppermint. Perhaps it's because I have from time to time felt a need to whack something with a hammer.

Have you ever had a day...or some days...like that? Times when the stress...and tension...and demands of the day were more than you could take? If only you had a peppermint pig to smash and feel the instant release, while at the same time soothing your frazzled nerves with the taste of peppermint and the promised bonus of good fortune yet to come, right?

I'm writing this at the beginning of the Christmas season, and as I think of the appeal of traditions and peppermint...and of the anxiety and stress that are also part of this time of year...the idea of the Peppermint Pig strikes a responsive chord. I think I like the idea of taking a positive action that will leave a good taste in everyone's mouth and hold the promise of good tidings for us all in the future.

Oh! That's right! That's what Christmas is all about, isn't it? At least it is for all Believers. Think about it for a minute.

At a time when all the world is under the threat of wars... and economic failure...and the danger of natural disaster...and overwhelming health concerns. In short, in a time when we all would welcome some positive action to bring us hope, we are once more reminded that God is aware of our trials and tribulations. That He has taken steps to save us from the doom which seems to be unavoidable.

You may not be able to have the emotional release that comes from smashing a Peppermint Pig, but this season you can at least break off a piece of one of those peppermint candy canes. And, each time you do, remember that God has good things in store for all who put their confidence in Him.

God has known since before the beginning of time the trials, opportunities and difficulties you would be...and are now...facing. The message He sent to shepherds by way of the angelic choir is the same one He has for you today: "Don't be afraid! We're here to let you know God has provided a way for you to meet His standards. A baby has been born who will grow up to show you the way. Go find Him and see for yourself."

He went to the trouble of sending His Son among us as a little Baby and then to promise us something better than "good luck" in the form of good tidings which shall be to all who love Him.

That's your challenge today...be like those shepherds and go find Jesus. Accept His promise of eternal blessing...then go and tell everyone you meet of the great thing which has come to pass.

One translation of Psalm 34:8 reads, "O taste and see how gracious the Lord is. Blest is the man who trusts in Him." That taste is a lot more satisfying than any size Peppermint Pig...and you don't need to use a hammer to get it, either.

PARABLE OF THE TWO-PART SOLUTION

For much of the last twenty years a substantial part of my livelihood has come from restoring, repairing and re-caning a large variety of chairs, rockers and wicker furniture. Over the last few years, I have avoided any complete stripping and refinishing projects, because of the space, equipment and effort they require.

For a lot longer than good Christian witness calls for, I have had in my shop a child's antique rocking chair. It was left in my care to be restored and was safely put away until I could get to it. That rocker and its patient and long-suffering owner have been on my mind lately, and I felt convicted—with the Holy Spirit speaking through my sweet wife Joyce—to quit putting it off and get the job done.

Thus inspired, I planned my attack on the project and set up my work space. Then I got out my dusty, trusty volume of *The Furniture Doctor*, by George Grotz, to refresh my memory as to the chemicals and formulas necessary for successful stripping. Since I have essentially been out of the refinishing business for a while, I have had to re-stock all the chemicals and materials needed.

The first step in restoring an antique of this sort is to remove all traces of the old finish. That requires the complete removal of the remaining lacquer or varnish, the stain, and the accumulated dirt and grime from decades of use. Next, since the stripping process plus the effects of aging tend to darken the wood, it is also necessary to use some sort of wood bleach to return it to its natural color.

Once the wood has been reconditioned, the next step is to stain it to the desired tone. Finally, one must apply the required number of coats of the final finish.

Over the years of teaching Sunday School classes, I have discussed the concept of forgiveness of sin, and that for Believers it is a once-in-a-lifetime event. The first question following that statement is usually, "Does that mean if we're Christians we can't sin?"

My stock answer to that question has usually been, "Of course, since we're still human we will still yield to sin, but once we become Christians, we're no longer able to enjoy sinning." That then begs the question, "If we can still sin, how is our forgiveness once and for all? Do we have to continually go back and confess? What if we forget to confess something, or commit a sin without knowing it? What then?"

I hope I'm not the only one who has had trouble finding a satisfactory response to that train of thought. However, as of this week I think I have found a way to illustrate the facts of forgiveness and continuous cleansing.

It was while reviewing formulas and securing the needed materials to prepare for that two-step procedure, that a recent Bible Study lesson popped into my mind. One of the key verses was one I had memorized many years ago, I John 1:9, "If we confess our sins, He is faithful and righteous to forgive us our sins and to cleanse us from all unrighteousness." (HCSB)

Here's what occurred to me. Just as one must decide that an antique chair needs its finish restored, one must accept the fact that he or she has said, done or thought things that displease God. That is a simple definition of the word sin.

When sin is confessed, God has promised to forgive that sin, because the penalty for that sin was paid in full by the sacrifice of Jesus.

There is no need to pay for it ever again. In the same way, the old finish on my chair is removed, the wood is restored to its original condition and the new finish is applied to provide permanent protection.

Finally, although there may be the accumulation of dirt, grease and grime on the newly restored finish, it can be repeatedly cleaned and polished without disturbing the permanent finish. Just so, although one may sin and fall short of God's glory numerous times, all that is needed by forgiven Believers is regular cleansing and polishing to keep redeemed souls in mint condition.

So, you see, for the redeemed, salvation is a two-step solution which restores and seals our souls for eternity, and then repeatedly cleanses us to keep us fit for God's daily service. The next time you dust your fine furniture let that serve as a reminder of how the Lord deals with you each and every day.

PARABLE OF THE SENDING TREE

What a wonderful age this is! A marvelous age of quick travel on wing, wheel or rail; of quick communication by phone, fax, FedEx or Facebook. An age when there's no need for us to get lost anywhere on the planet, what with that gentle, long-suffering voice that urges us to "Turn now," or "Make a U-turn at the next opportunity," when we fail to heed her advice. (Of course, I'm talking about my GPS, which I have named Annie, and not my faithful, loving wife and navigator Joyce, since I *always* heed her advice.)

This is an age when communication can be amazingly close to instant—at least, as instantly as our digits can search out and tap the keys on our keyboards and touchscreens. We can send the most breathtaking photographs hurtling through the ether more quickly than we can think of tags to attach to them.

People can show their faces, and anything else they think of, to friends and friends-of-friends-of friends; they can text and Instant Message and Tweet faster than the time it takes to stop and consider whether what they're passing on is worth the readers' time, or even prudent to share.

Don't misunderstand me. I'm in favor of these conveniences made possible in this electronic, digital, Internet age. I Google, e-mail and text, and even Facebook on occasion. And whenever my children or grandchildren can show me how, I'll place things in my Dropbox and disperse them into the Cloud—wherever that is.

I hadn't really thought too much about how I had become accustomed to these things until recently. I've written about spending time relaxing and being inspired by the lovely vistas to be seen from the comfortable porch at the Powell Farm retreat in Walland, Tennessee.

My Joyce was taking part in a family event in Knoxville and left me there to enjoy the quiet and peaceful atmosphere. As I sat, soaking in the sounds of the pastoral silence, I thought, "I guess this might be a good time to let the family back in Marietta know we arrived okay and that all is well." That's when I ran headlong into one of the perplexing problems of this age of instant communication. There was no cell phone service. No bars...for those who know what that means.

I was not in a panic—I'm at an age where I reserve panic for really urgent situations—but I was faced with a problem that had me stymied. How does one E, IM or TXT when there's no cell phone or Wi-fi service?

Well, Marshall Powell came to the rescue with true, old-time country wisdom and know-how. He said, "There's a place out in the back yard just past the driveway where you can get service on a good day. Go stand by that big oak tree and I think you should be able to call from there."

Before I go further, let me assure you that the Powell Farm does have traditional telephone service, and even television and Internet service for anyone who is old-school enough to prefer them. It's just that cell phone coverage is too thin to be what "city folks" are used to.

Anyway...I walked across the driveway and a nicely manicured expanse of lawn to the "sending tree" and tried again to make my call. After a little experimentation, I found that if I faced slightly to the northeast, leaned against the tree and extended my left foot to the side, I could get as many as two bars and successfully pass word back to family in the civilized world.

I'm exaggerating, but Marshall was right on target with the fact that the sending tree was in exactly the prime location to pick up the only available cell signal in that vicinity. And it was all the signal I needed to get through to the folks at home.

As I picture that sending tree there in Tennessee, I'm reminded that there are times in my life when I've felt it necessary to go through all sorts of steps and procedures to communicate with God. We all have our spiritual sending trees, don't we? It may be that special prayer closet, or posture, or just the right combination of holy words that we think are necessary to put us in touch with the Father, but whichever ones we favor, we have them and depend on them from time to time.

Over the years of walking with Him I have learned an important lesson, and perhaps you have, too. I never need to go stand by any sending tree in order to send my prayers—or to receive His answers, either, for that matter. His Spirit is beside and within me as I go, wherever I go.

The Lord hears me whether I'm in the solitude of my study or His sanctuary, if I'm doing the speed limit on the interstate or pausing thoughtfully in the grocery store aisle. Whether I'm in my natural habitat or in a far-off foreign land, He is there.

You can seek out your favorite sending tree if you prefer, but remember there is no sending tree as dear to the father as the one right there in a Believer's heart. You can meet Him at that sending tree any time you want. How about right now?

PARABLE OF THE WOODPECKER AND THE HONEYBEE

I'll begin by saying that I'm not an ornithologist, entomologist, botanist, archeologist, or mathematician. If you happen to be learned in any of these disciplines, and take issue with any of my observations, I welcome your enlightened opinions.

Second, in case you're new to my Parables, I want to also warn you that I am an unabashed Creationist. I agree with those who argue that an orderly creation is the product of an all-knowing, all-wise, all-powerful Creator we call God. He calls Himself "I Am."

If those details don't bother you, then let's proceed with the Parable of The Woodpecker and the Honeybee.

It was many years ago that I first heard a radio commentator reveal some interesting facts about the family of birds commonly called woodpeckers. He began by stating that the woodpecker's prominent proboscis, or bill, is perhaps its most obvious and identifiable physical characteristic.

All birds have a bill, of course, used to probe for, crush, hold and carry bits of food. However, in addition to performing those functions well, the bill of the woodpecker has a unique dual purpose. First, the woodpecker, while clinging to the side of a tree, taps vigorously on the bark as the bird listens for any sign of movement inside the survey area.

If a few taps stir sounds inside the bark, the bill becomes a pile-driver, drilling in and digging out the insect morsel formerly dwelling inside. I also suspect there's something special about the ability to hear grubs squirming around under several millimeters of bark.

It takes specially designed and coordinated muscles to tap quickly and with enough force to penetrate the surface. Just try tapping on your forehead as rapidly as the tapping of a woodpecker on a tree and you'll see what I mean.

The skull of the woodpecker is also uniquely equipped for this tapping/drilling process. Our woodpecker friend has a thick layer of cartilage which cushions the force of the pounding, protecting the skull and brain of the creature. How many of its pre-historic ancestors died of broken bills and crushed skulls, I wonder, before one had the wisdom to grow this extra padding?

Many other features of the woodpecker make it unique. As far as scientists have determined, none of these abilities had anything to do with the ability of the woodpecker to survive. Why, then, would they have developed? And why don't all birds have them? Hmmmmm.

Another of my favorite case-studies regarding the theory of evolution is that of the lowly honeybee. What is astounding to me is the assertion of the dyed-in-the-wool evolutionist that these tiny wonders evolved over billions of years.

I cannot begin to imagine the multiplied billions of years needed to produce the first honeybee, with its many unique features. Then, consider that entomologists tell us the honeybee cannot exist alone. The typical healthy hive of honeybee's numbers in the thousands, averaging from 20,000 to 40,000 in a hive.

Evolutionists mock the faith of believers in a Creator. Yet they seem to have no difficulty believing in the random combination of atoms, molecules and cells to produce—at the same time and in the same place—the multiplied thousands of these specialized insects necessary to sustain a successful hive.

The honeybee community is also amazing to me. At daylight each and every day a band of these tireless workers exits the hive in all directions, searching for their preferred nourishment, the pollen of various blossoms. Whenever one of these faithful fliers finds a promising food source, it returns directly to the hive, even though it might be quite a distance away, certainly out of sight.

Upon its return it performs a directional dance, informing other gatherers of the location of the new discovery, and the army departs to bring in the life-sustaining goods. Just think of the countless bees that got lost and died, the countless hives that starved and collapsed before they developed their ingenious HPS (Hive Positioning Systems)—if one chooses to accept the Theory of Evolution as fact.

However, finding the life-giving pollen is only the beginning. Once the pollen has been collected the processing begins. Here's where the specialized digestive systems enter in. Some of the honeybees process the pollen to produce the wax-like material needed to construct the hive itself, engineering perfectly hexagonal cells, all connected and stacked in the most compact and structurally sound manner possible. Trial and error can't explain how they learned to make wax, or how to use it to make a hexagon, because discovery of a faulty, failed hive hasn't been reported.

Other workers process the pollen and produce honey, to feed the members of the hive, with enough left over to share with anyone brave enough to obtain it from the hive. Still other workers process the same pollen to produce a special, high energy version to be fed to the queen honeybee so she can use her specially-designed reproductive system to lay thousands of eggs to produce the thousands of honeybees needed to sustain the hive.

The woodpecker and the honeybee are only two of the countless creatures that argue for acceptance of the idea of an all-wise and all-powerful Designer and Creator. I believe that it takes a lot more faith

to imagine that these things developed by chance, from ooze that had no origin, which resulted from the explosion of previously non-existent matter.

If you have never met the Creator, I'd be glad to arrange an introduction. He's a personal friend of mine. He knows all about you, and He really does want to meet you.

PARABLE OF GOOD THINGS

When I was in the advertising business, we did brochures and mailers for a gentleman who sold advertising specialties. You know...those imprinted pens, note pads, coffee mugs and other "freebies" that companies hand out to promote their name, business or product.

He always left a variety of samples in his wake as he made his way through the office. I must have a tote bag full of them here in the house somewhere. There was one pen in particular that he handed out in abundance, almost every time he came around. Its imprint read, "The five greatest words: I WOKE UP THIS MORNING."

I think of that imprint frequently when someone greets me with "How are you doing today?" I will often say, "The good news is, I woke up this morning." I recently heard a response with a similar sentiment. When greeted, the old-timer said, "Well, I woke up on the green side of the lawn." What both of these responses have in common is that they're based upon the assumption that before we can hope for a good outcome for the day's activities, there must be a good beginning.

All our lives we are coached on the importance of a good beginning. "A job well begun is half done." "There's no substitute for a good first impression." "You've got to put your best foot forward." And other maxims about a good beginning being essential to a successful result.

Yet, no matter how good a start we make on each of the projects in life, it's a fact that we usually get so caught up in the continuing action that we often breeze right through the good things of life without considering just how good they are until the best has passed. Only then do we come to appreciate them. That's why we are often admonished to "Stop and smell the roses" as we go, instead of wistfully trying to recall their fragrance after they're gone.

To the young, youth drags by, and they chafe under the burden of unexpected, unwelcome and unfamiliar everyday experiences. Yet those young carefree years are viewed with fondness and nostalgia through the lens of maturity. "Ahhh...the good old days!" we say.

I remember clearly one family vacation we took when I was a boy. My mother's best friend from Robertsdale High School invited us to spend a week with her family in their beach house on the Alabama Gulf Shore. Weeks of planning and packing were accomplished, the laborious drive was over, and we pulled up to the stilt-mounted cottage by the sand dunes.

While the adults unloaded the car and got settled in, I kicked off my shoes and socks and ran with abandon over the dune and down onto the beach for my very first view of the ocean. I spent every possible minute on the sand, in the surf and playing pirate games among the dunes. Each day held new adventures...new discoveries... new challenges. I learned to deal with sunburn, mosquitoes the size of pigeons, and sand spurs that lay in wait and attacked me as I innocently invaded their domain.

Before I knew it the week was gone, the car was packed and everyone was loaded in...except me. I was still down on the beach, stubbornly refusing to admit it was time to leave. I didn't want that good week to be over. A generation later my girls were the same way. It was only with great reluctance that they came dragging from that last wade in the surf, wishing that the good times at Pawleys Island could go on and on.

But we have all been chastised with the adage "All good things must come to an end." And so, they must. It seems that the true test of a good thing, is how quickly it seems to pass, and how much we are startled by—and unwilling to accept—its ending.

Perhaps, like me, you enjoy attending plays, musicals and operas. Each time I go with eagerness and anticipation, and I'm a little sad when it is over, and it's time to go home. If it is a really good show, the sadness is greater. But that is the time when I am moved to show my appreciation for having been shown a really good time...that's the time for a standing ovation.

Now...here's my advice about experiencing the good things of life. Wake up in the morning, intending to grab hold of the day and make a good start of it. Go into the day with excitement and enthusiasm, look for the good things that await your attention and participation. Enjoy each experience...laugh a lot and get others laughing with you... that guarantees that you'll discover more good things than you could have imagined. Share them with as many others as you can. Help them understand why they are good.

And when it's time for each of the good things to end, as they surely will, show your appreciation with a rousing standing ovation. Remember that you can't go on to the next good thing until you have let go of the one that is finished. Then wake up the next morning...go out and begin looking for the next good thing the Lord has in store for you, and start all over again.

PARABLE OF
REGRETS ONLY

I t's not unusual for me to wake up in the morning with a song playing in the back room of my mind, like some radio left on while I was out of the house. What seemed a little peculiar this morning was the particular song that was "on" as I arose.

"Miss Otis regrets she's unable to lunch today, Madam..."

Now, even though that novelty song by Cole Porter has been recorded many times by the likes of Nat "King" Cole, Bette Midler and Ella Fitzgerald...and even was referred to by Agatha Christie in one of her Mrs. Marple mysteries..."Miss Otis Regrets" isn't one of those songs one is likely to hum while going about one's household chores. I'd even be a little surprised to learn that you have even heard of it.

In a learned pronouncement from atop Mount Wikipedia, I read that this quirky song was written in 1935 by Mr. Porter for one of those musical revues that were so popular in the day, and was quite a hit. In his terse style he tells the sad tale of a socialite, Miss Otis, who after being seduced and then cruelly rejected, hunts down her seducer in Lovers' Lane, shoots him, is arrested and then lynched by a mob. Before she becomes a tree ornament, she recites the line reported by her servant, "Miss Otis regrets she's unable to lunch today, Madam."

I heard a rendition of "Miss Otis" recently on a broadcast of "On the Town," a regular PBS program produced by Musical Theater Heritage which highlights music and background stories from Twentieth Century Broadway musicals. The clip played by George Harter was from a very humorous recitation by Noel Coward recorded many years ago.

Anyway...I don't know how that button on my mental jukebox got pushed, but that's what was playing this morning. As I sat down to write, that was the theme that had captured my thoughts.

I imagined the socially proper Miss Otis, perhaps standing on a rock or a stump, with the noose around her neck...pausing briefly before meeting her demise to instruct her servant to convey her regrets at having to miss lunch with an acquaintance. How ludicrous that seems, right?

However, as I sit here composing my thoughts, having heard only a few hours ago that a good friend from our old Sunday School class has just graduated into the Kingdom, I'm trying to imagine what his last conscious thoughts might have been. He had much to be grateful for and many accomplishments for which he'll be remembered... wonderful family...loving and faithful friends. But I can't help but wonder if he, like Miss Otis, would have expressed regrets if given the chance.

A favorite device of dramatists is to use the death-bed statements of a key character to make some crucial moral point or lead to the resolution of whatever crisis is to be faced. I'm not sure why the "If Only's" portrayed in those sentimental scenes are so depressing... unless it's because they are a reminder that we all have actions and failures in our lives which we regret and intend to correct before our time is up. If only we had advance warning that our time was about to run out.

Dad told me many times that the only times he ever heard his step-father—the gentle Southern gentleman we called "Podnuh" (Partner)—use bad words was when he said, "You should live your life so that you can walk down the street and tell any man you meet to go to hell," and "I don't care if you can't be anything but a garbage man... just be the best damn garbage man there is."

Isn't that just a couple of ways to say one should live life in such a way that when it's over there won't be any regrets? A tall order, I know...impossible, perhaps...but isn't that a worthy goal?

I have good news for you. The Lord has promised to all who accept Him that He will make it possible for us to live that kind of life...such that, even if the world puts a noose around our neck, we can stand firm, knowing that He has paid for our faults. Unlike Miss Otis, we'll have no regrets.

PARABLE OF THE BLIND DATE THEORY

I consider the years I spent as a college student at Georgia Tech as golden. I learned many deep and profound lessons while I was there...a considerable number of which were without benefit of professor, classroom or textbook.

As I think back, I realize that so many of my current ideals and values were developed during those times. Not all of these are important or profound, of course. In fact, many of them are quite trivial...matters of little consequence to anyone but myself. However, some of them have had a significant influence on my philosophy of life.

For example, I recall one occasion when I was relaxing at the fraternity house between classes. Two fraternity brothers were engaged in a spirited discussion of deep social significance. The question was whether or not one of them should allow himself to be set up with a blind date.

The first brother had met a girl he wanted to date, but she wouldn't go out with him unless he could find a suitable recruit to date her best friend, so they could double-date. So...here he was, offering his most persuasive arguments to engage his roommate for the assignment.

After many long and logical points in favor of accepting the challenge, he delivered his final and strongest. "Any idiot can have fun on a blind date, knowing that he doesn't ever need to see that person again unless he wants to. There's simply nothing to lose." Apparently, that did the trick.

I've remembered and applied that advice many times during my life. Not so much as a rule for social behavior as a challenge to take a chance on something new...to risk venturing into unfamiliar, uncharted territory. After all, there are a lot of instances in life when the only reason for *not* trying something unknown is...well, simply that it *is* unknown.

Have you ever considered how many opportunities you may have overlooked or ignored only because they represented something seemingly strange or different? How often have you been like the boys in the commercial, refusing to try something and offering it to "Mikey" because he'll try anything. Only if Mikey likes it will they give it a taste.

During the 1960's and '70's, naturalist Euell Gibbons wrote a series of books, beginning with "Stalking the Wild Asparagus," which promoted seeking out and preparing foods collected from shrubs, plants and roots commonly found in the wild. He was definitely in favor of discovering and trying things that were unusual and unknown.

However, Gibbons gave this advice, "You don't just go around eating strange things and waiting to see if you die." Even this idea of "Try it, you'll like it" has to be applied with an ample dose of common sense. But few of our life challenges ever turn out to be life *or death* challenges, do they? Many are opportunities to test different ways of thinking or acting that may be rewarding.

There's another side to this "Blind Date Theory" that I haven't thought too much about, but which also shapes many of our experiences. A lot of times it is easier to accept a blind date than it is to take a chance with someone who already knows us...and knows *about* us. Sometimes we feel more vulnerable with those already acquainted with us than we do with strangers.

In workshops for Christians in personal witnessing, there is a diagram called Concentric Circles of Concern. It shows those levels of concern with "Self" at the center, radiating outward through "Family," "Friends," "Acquaintances," etc., to the outermost circle, labeled "Person X."

It's interesting, isn't it, that whenever we think of sharing the Gospel with others, we automatically think of Person X as the prime target? That's a direct application of the Blind Date Theory: There's no risk of failure when you never need to see that person again unless you want to.

Don't get me wrong...we should all be prepared to love Person X and want to share with him or her the blessings of life with Jesus in charge. But what about those in our inner circles...those people we know and who know us...many of whom we love and for whom we care dearly?

Surely, the risk from rejection is greater...and we must expect to associate with them over a longer period of time. Can you, though, think of anything more joyful in life than to be able to live it with those with whom you have in common the hope and promise of Eternal Life?

So, here's the observation of Foo Foo the Wise: Enjoy the occasional spiritual Blind Date with Person X when the challenge arises, but make a regular practice of engaging those family members, friends and acquaintances you encounter each day. Never neglect the opportunity to invite them into the Kingdom with you. Those are Dates you'll always remember.

PARABLE OF THE BLOSSOMS OF SPRING

Not too long ago I experienced one of modern technology's most traumatic events. My computer crashed. It died unceremoniously and completely. There were no long and lingering farewells...no warning rattles, whirs or pops. Not even the dreaded "blue screen of death." It just went to sleep one night and never awoke. Very sad.

That was the bad news. The good news was that I was able to get a good buy on a new machine, and, with the able assistance of my son-in-law, got it up and running within a few days. Of course, because I'm not a certified member of the computer generation I am still trying to learn how to get it house-broken for my uses.

One of the features of the new operating system that I usually don't pay much attention to is a band along one side of the desktop screen that shows the current weather, time, calendar and an on-going slide show from my extensive Pictures file. It was one of those pictures that caught my attention the other day and started me thinking.

I can't remember the special occasion, but one of our daughters sent a lovely spring flower arrangement to my wife. We enjoyed their fragrance and extravagant beauty for days. They stayed on display several days past their prime, because we just couldn't bear to throw them out.

My trusty digital camera preserved their lovely colors—our increasingly faulty memories were pressed into service to preserve their exotic perfume. However, eventually the blossoms dried out and the leaves and petals turned brown and dropped off, and they went into the trash.

From the first buds that thrust their heads through frost-crusted earth in late Winter, to the full-blown blossoms that compete for our admiration on into the early days of Summer, there is a continuous cycle of color and aroma...something to please even the most cynical curmudgeon. In an unrivaled variety show, produced and directed by the Creator, each species stages its two-week performance as if trying to upstage all the others. Then its blossoms bow and exit stage right. That's it for the "blossoms that bloom in the Spring...tra-la." Then the grand curtain falls and we await the next scene.

Act Two isn't nearly so exciting or entertaining. Just a lot of green leaves and shoots. Some crops to be cultivated...some weeds to be yanked out and disposed of. Generally speaking, Act Two isn't a lot of fun. Not a lot of applause to be heard as summer blends into Fall.

But then there's Act Three, and we begin to understand the purpose of it all. The awaking of the seeds in the Prologue...the blooming of blossoms in Act One...the greening of stems, leaves and fruits in Act Two...all culminate with the ripening of all the various fruits. Yes, even the beautiful flowers in the Spring bouquet exist for the purpose of bearing fruit, even if that is only the seeds and bulbs necessary to produce more blossoms to beautify succeeding Springs.

There's a striking graphic demonstration of the meaning of life that can be found in the Parable of the Blossoms of Spring. We applaud the symbol of birth represented by the bud, and of a purposeful life in the blossom. We are saddened by the wilting that follows and have a sense of loss when they are turned into compost. It is all too easy to mourn their passing, forgetting that they are not lost...merely that they have completed their purpose and left behind all that is necessary for the production of the fruit for which they were ordained by The Master Gardener.

Remember the lesson of the Parable of The Blossoms of Spring: Death is not the end of life, but merely the passing from one stage of life to another. And that the true measure of the success of a life is the quality of the fruit that springs up after it is long gone. The more attractive the blossom, the more effective the pollination and the better nourished the fruit.

So, to put it briefly, grow where you're planted...bloom like crazy...and leave the fruit production and harvest to the practiced Hand of the Divine Master Gardener.

PARABLE OF THE LOWLY SNAIL

My mostly-Black-Lab, Suzy Q Mahoney, and I were out for our morning constitutional the other day and approached a neighbor who was sitting on the curb by his mailbox, planting and un-planting flowers. In his lap was his two-year-old grandson, "helping him from his work."

As my companion and I drew near, she and the little boy seemed to be drawn to each other. In his delight and childish curiosity, he smiled and reached out to touch her. In her characteristic enthusiasm she pulled forward on the lead so she could give him a few excited licks on the hand.

He wasn't too sure about her animated approach and those moist gestures of friendship, however. His smile quickly vanished and his hand was withdrawn as he retreated to the safety of his grandfather's arms.

After the grandfather and I had exchanged pleasantries, and Suzy and I resumed our rounds, I thought about how quickly the little boy's instinctive behavior had changed. "He pulled that little hand back as fast as a snail's tentacle recoils when it touches an obstacle," I observed to myself.

That was all it took to get my subconscious in gear as we completed our walk.

I began replaying old mental videos of childhood days, whenever I would come across a snail during my play...of the natural revulsion to that creepy, slimy creature as it slowly oozed its way along...of the boyish, irresistible urge to touch it. Yuck! Then touch it again, just for good measure.

The feature that was most intriguing, though, was the way it reacted whenever one touched its antenna...actually its tentacle...or what I referred to as its antler. I couldn't get enough amusement out of the way that "antler" disappeared when I touched it. No matter how many times I repeated the action, the result was the same: I would touch it...it would recoil and completely withdraw...then it would slowly extend again a few seconds later.

Those childhood memories wouldn't turn off when our trek was ended. I later found myself Googling (or was it Yahooing? I'm never quite sure.) "Snails." In this remarkable age of the internet, I was instantly inundated with more information than I could ever exhaust...more than I ever wanted to know...about the wonderful world of snaildom.

For instance, the title "snail" is generally used to refer to all those "molluscan members of the class Gastropoda." Or that snails are second only to insects in number and variety among all the earth's creatures. How about the fact that they are hermaphrodites, meaning that they each have both male and female reproductive organs? And did you know that slimy mucous trail is what makes it possible for them to cling to any type of surface, just like wetting the surface of a suction cup increases its ability to adhere, even to a non-porous surface? I also learned that the typical garden snail zips along at the breezy speed of 55 YPH (Yards Per Hour). Breathtaking, huh?

Yes, writers on the marvelous worldwide web have rhapsodized megabytes of data dedicated to the subject of the lowly snail.

But...back to the original thought that raised the whole subject: The reaction of that antler...excuse me, that tentacle...and the way it blindly reaches for information and suddenly withdraws when it comes into contact with something unfamiliar. That is such a human response, isn't it? We see it, unguarded and without deceit, in children, of course, but it is also completely common to adults as well...albeit not always quite so obviously demonstrated.

Have you ever noticed how people respond to the approach of the dirty, disheveled, apparently homeless person on the street? Or to the young person with holes in his or her jeans...with strange haircuts and colors...tatoos and piercings. How about those who speak a strange language or follow an unattractive lifestyle? Don't your tentacles tend to withdraw...even a little bit?

Dad used to tell me, "Anybody can be friendly to the lovely people." But it takes a genuine Christian spirit to fight that natural TWS (Tentacle Withdrawal Syndrome) as Jesus challenges us to befriend the friendless...and, yes, even the unfriendly...to love the unlovely and unlovable.

The lowly snail reacts to what it perceives as an unknown threat, and thus defends itself by protecting its sensitive organs. However, when we respond in that same instinctive way, we're usually defending personal preferences, not against genuine threats to our safety and well-being.

A famous writer was quoted as saying, "It is better to be sometimes cheated than to fail to trust." I would add that it is better to be sometimes hurt than to be like the lowly snail and withdraw from possible contact with others, who may, in fact, enrich our lives and give us an opportunity to demonstrate a genuine Christian witness. For, as Jesus said, "...ye do it unto me."

PARABLE OF THE PASSING STORM

In "Parable of A Summer's Lightning" I wrote about how my dad helped me overcome my fear of Nature's boisterous fireworks displays...how some of my most peaceful moments since that experience have come while contemplating the coming and passing of seasonal thunderstorms.

I've spent countless hours sitting enraptured on the porch of a rented beach cottage, watching storm clouds swapping instant messages of heat lightning back and forth across the horizon. I get as much satisfaction from that as the current generation of TV fanatics gets from watching episodes of "American Idol" or "So You Think You Can Dance?".

My sweet wife Lyn, on the other hand, was always the family's Weather Worrier. While I sat on the porch absorbing the sights and sounds of a passing storm, she was most often found huddled near the TV or weather radio anticipating the terrors that storm might wield over us and those dear to us. She was ready to pack up and head for the storm cellar at any moment.

At home, Lyn had a place prepared in a safe corner of our basement which we could use as a refuge whenever the storm sirens in the neighborhood sounded...complete with battery-operated TV and radio, and provisions to sustain us if and when the threatened disaster should strike.

There is no phobia so bizarre, no paranoia so irrational, however, that there isn't some degree of justification. I was reminded of that during the weather events that have struck the Southeast recently, destroying homes and businesses, killing and injuring many.

There's no denying that countless lives have been preserved as a result of the persistent and thorough reporting of TV and radio weather gurus and their determination to cover...often in excruciating detail...every aspect of each storm cell as it materializes, approaches and departs. To one who finds himself in the path of one of these weather events, this exhaustive coverage is valuable, reassuring and, often, lifesaving.

As I find myself now cast in the role of family Weather Watcher... if not Worrier...I realize that I pay a lot closer attention to the weather coverage than I used to. I can't sit and enjoy the developing reports with quite the same carefree abandon as I once did.

In fact, as this current storm formed and made its way East, I was more and more alert with each interruption of regular programming for periodic updates. For several hours I kept my computer on-line, continually updating the weather radar loop, so I could keep informed of just how far away the yellow, red and purple blobs were from the arrow that indicated my position. I was fascinated by the recognition that the yellow mass touched my location marker just as I heard the raindrops begin lashing at the window of my study.

I went to sleep, finally, with the TV on...weather whisperers droning in the background...trusting that something would wake me should the threatened disaster become a reality. What did bring me back to consciousness was the somewhat calmer tone of Weather Woman announcing that the storm was now passing away to the Northeast leaving most us at last in peace, albeit with many others facing the unpleasant reality of having to pick up the pieces left in its wake.

One of the unavoidable assurances of existence is that you and I will each have to deal with the storms of life. Sometimes they will come unannounced...occasionally they will be devastating...at other times they will pass harmlessly...but they will almost always be memorable.

How prepared are you for the storms of life?

As I studied the screen showing the approaching storm cells last night, I couldn't help but recall the words of a gospel song "'til the Storm Passes By," written by Mosie Lister. The quartet I sing with, The Singing Deacons, has presented it many times. Let me share the lyrics with you:

"In the dark of the midnight have I oft hid my face,

While the storms howl above me, and there's no hiding place.

'Mid the crash of the thunder, Precious Lord, hear my cry,

'Keep me safe 'til the storm passes by.'

'Til the storm passes over, 'til the thunder sounds no more,

'til the clouds roll forever from the sky,

Hold me fast, let me stand in the hollow of Thy hand;

Keep me safe 'til the storm passes by."

So...I can still enjoy the experience of seasonal storms and at the same time be prepared to take precautions should there be a genuine threat. But don't worry about me when the storms rage, because the Lord has the part of me that is immortal safe in the hollow of His hand. Safe 'til the storm passes by. Can you say the same? If not, I'd be glad to help you get weatherproofed. Just ask.

PARABLE OF THE CHILD-PROOF HOUSE

Over the years I have observed an interesting trend that seems to be increasing at an amazing rate as time passes. I noticed it for the first time when I first became a parent and realized that, unlike automobiles, lawnmowers, dishwashers...even radios and CD players...babies didn't come with any kind of Owner's Manual. We looked for some authority to guide us as new parents.

Lyn and I did what many young parents of the fifties and sixties did. We rushed out and bought a copy of Dr. Spock's book on raising kids. Oh, I know...Dr. Spock got involved in a lot of things outside his field, and has taken some controversial stands on things since those years, but back then he was considered the guru of child rearing.

Frankly, I can't remember a lot of what we read about how to be parents...and there may be a lot that I have recalled inaccurately... but there are some of his pronouncements as an authority on children that seemed to make sense. For instance, he said it's normal for babies to cry. They cry when they're hungry, wet, uncomfortable or in pain... but they also cry when they merely want attention, or to be held and be comforted.

Dr. Spock said that if the parent responds to every whimper and cry it's a great disservice to the child, because it teaches that the world is at the child's beck and call...that he or she will never learn to distinguish between the important and the trivial needs in life. When left alone for long enough, a child will learn to cope with the trivial things, and seek help only for those that are important. His advice: If an infant cries for more than ten or fifteen minutes, go see what's wrong, otherwise you're only training yourself.

Another Spock-ism that I remember is that it's important to child-proof your home...but only up to a point. Of course, keep those sharp, pointy things out of a toddler's reach. Block off stairways and keep certain doors latched. Those are just common sense.

But, unless I'm mistaken, he was more in favor of house-proofing your child. Begin early to teach what places and things are off-limits and forbidden. And *enforce* those rules.

In his story "The Man Who Corrupted Hadleyburg," Mark Twain tells of a town the citizens of which had such a sterling reputation for honesty that their trustworthiness was taken for granted. No one ever even considered trying to tempt them. They lost their ability to resist temptation, because it was never tested, until one day when a stranger came to town. When faced with genuine temptation, they were quickly overcome.

When our children were small, Lyn and I didn't follow the conventional wisdom of the day and move everything up and out of their reach, like those trying to protect their valuables from a flood. We expended most of our efforts in teaching them which things were all right for them to touch and play with and which ones weren't. And with few exceptions that philosophy was successful. And we stuck with that policy except when our friends brought their children to the house.

Now...back to the disturbing trend I was talking about. Am I the only one to notice that the tendency today is to attempt to "world-proof" our children as well as our adults?

Don't dare go out of the house without your safety glasses, elbow- and knee-pads and safety helmet securely in place. Don't even think about picking up a tool or implement without first checking the warning notices attached. "Warning: This ax has sharp edges that can be harmful, and may result in the severing of body parts if not used properly." "Notice: This ladder is intended for reaching high places. However, falling from those high places has been known to result in injury." "Possible side effects of this drug are chapped lips, paper cuts and occasional sudden death."

It has become apparent to me that what we once called common sense is no longer all that common. Or at least many of those who have adopted the mantle of Defender of the Simple-minded seem to think so. Their answer is to throw a fence around anything that could possibly be misused by the selfish, the ignorant, the careless and the foolish among us to protect them from harm.

Is it any mystery why Prohibition didn't work? We have laws against drug use, speeding and prostitution, but those don't work so well, either, do they? Why do you suppose that is?

The fact is that we can't child-proof our world any more than we can child-proof our homes with any degree of success, because of human nature. If anyone could succeed at this approach, God could, don't you agree? But all you need to do is look around you to see how it worked for Him.

God gave only a few simple rules: "Love Me. Love those around you. Demonstrate that love by your actions each day. Follow these directions and you can be with Me in My kingdom." Do we follow those rules consistently? No, we do not.

Jesus told us that God didn't intend to put a fence around every little thing that could harm us, or separate us from Him. His plan was for us to world-proof ourselves by establishing those boundaries internally, so we could enjoy the beauty and the bounty of His creation as He intended.

Child-proof your home the best you can. Rely on the authorities to child-proof the world as much as possible. But always remember

that there is no substitute for home- and world-proofing your child by teaching them self-discipline, restraint and common sense before you turn them loose amid the charms and temptations of a sinful world.

Oh. And it's also not too late for you to apply that same principle to your own life.

PARABLE OF THE COUNTERTOP

Have you tried to sell any real estate lately? Whether you have or not, I'm sure you're aware that the economic conditions determine if it will be a "buyers' market" or a "sellers' market." Right now, we happen to be in a buyers' market.

When there are a lot of houses on the market, the buyers can shop around...they can be picky about details like paint colors and everything from minor to major repairs and touch-ups...they can bargain for a better price or get concessions on things like appliances and fixtures.

When we had trouble attracting buyers to my mother-in-law's condo, we decided to upgrade the kitchen appliances and fixtures to see if that would make it more appealing. After all, it was competing with newer and more modern ones in the same price range and located not too far away.

The new, brushed stainless steel finish really looks good...the range, refrigerator, dishwasher and microwave/range hood completely change the appearance of the kitchen. Now we're anticipating the final touch: new granite countertops.

You may have seen the ads on TV. Genuine granite is crushed, mixed with a polymer binder and formed into a product that boasts all the best features of granite, plus the lightness, durability and non-porous quality of the man-made polymer.

Each new countertop is made to order and fits neatly, seamlessly and perfectly over the old one. The old top is still there, but now it has been completely covered over and is out of sight. No major remodeling, repair or refurbishing necessary. No muss, no fuss.

As I sit here thinking about what the finished kitchen will look like, I can't help comparing it with the way the Holy Spirit works in the life of a new believer.

As one goes through life, the pressures of daily living, with its selfish choices and the defiling results of yielding to the sinful nature, take a toll on one's "shelf appeal." In Biblical terms, sin degrades the soul and makes it worthless for use in serving God.

Then Jesus comes along with an offer to restore that soul to a satisfying and useful condition. He offers a new nature...attractive, seamless, non-porous, impervious to scratches, scrapes, cracks, dents and dings.

Don't misunderstand...the Old Nature is still under there, and is still a threat to our daily thoughts and inclinations, but it has been made new by the on laying of the New Nature. Just like that countertop, we are rendered useful, our appearance is made appealing to those around us...and with that new covering we become presentable before God.

Can we still sin? Still have wicked thoughts? Still fall short of God's plan for us? Of course. But we are no longer held hostage by those sinful and wicked failures. No more are we victims of the original sin nature, but we are set free from the temporary satisfaction that yielding to sin once brought. We recover more quickly from occasional relapses into wickedness.

Have you had your spiritual countertop replaced? If not, I'm a certified representative of the manufacturer, and I'd be glad to discuss all the benefits with you, and help take care of all the details. I promise the installation is quick and easy. And it's already paid for. Such a deal.

PARABLE OF THE SEEING EYE

I wrote recently about growing up following the life and love of that naive but handsome hillbilly from Dogpatch, U.S.A, Li'l Abner. He had broad shoulders, a narrow waist and muscles that would be the envy of any of today's body builders. He had Elvis's hair before Elvis was cool, and his bib overalls always had one shoulder strap unfastened.

Li'l Abner Yokum was an uncomplicated young man, cast somewhat in the style of the silent movie hero, whose "strength is as the strength of ten, because his heart is pure." Abner's feisty mother, Mammy Yokum, clearly was the matriarch of the Yokum clan, and although she barely came up to his waist, she was capable of taking him to the woodshed when it was called for.

In her beat-up hat, striped stockings and high-buttoned shoes, with her corncob pipe clasped firmly between her teeth, there was hardly any problem or difficulty Mammy wouldn't light into... and hardly anybody she couldn't whip, or whip into line. She was overflowing with mountain wisdom, and, when circumstances called for it she could conjure up visions to guide future actions.

Often, she would draw on that wisdom or those visions and share these profound insights with Li'l Abner, and she would end with the phrase "...as any fool can plainly see." Abner's bemused response was always: "Ah see."

Have you ever thought about that simple expression, "I see."? We use it in a lot of ways, and it has a number of meanings, depending upon the circumstances.

Sometimes "I see..." is the beginning of a simple declarative sentence indicating that we have made visual contact with a physical object. At other times we use it as an expression of our imagination, probing the past or future and populating them with ideas of how things were or can become. "Dreaming dreams and seeing visions," as the prophet wrote. (Joel 2:28)

I recall the first time I saw one of those 3-D puzzles, where you gaze at a pattern or design long enough, and at just the right distance and just the right angle...and suddenly you can make out shapes and figures that seem to jump off the page. You *see* the hidden image.

Often the phrase indicates a moment of enlightenment and understanding...when one has been able to embrace a concept or principle with one's mind, and it becomes clear. I suppose the current street expression for that would be something like, "I feel you, bro."

What kinds of things keep us from "seeing"?

Sometimes it is something as simple as a lack of light. In a study of Physics, one learns that light must reflect off an object in order to be seen by the physical eye. If the light is not sufficient, or if there is not a reflective surface, there is no seeing.

There is another sense, however, in which there must be a mental frame of reference in order for the brain to identify the objective and formulate a response to the thing or idea so revealed. Without that there can be no understanding...no comprehension...no seeing.

The Bible uses the concept of seeing in both senses. The people wanted to *see* Jesus...to *see* God...the *see* the Kingdom. They wanted to satisfy their curiosity.

The Pharisees knew the Law, but didn't comprehend or accept the fact of Jesus, the Lawgiver in human form. Not the facts of His existence, which they could see, but rather His authority as God's Son. They "knew Him not." (John 1:10) They looked at Him without seeing.

Matthew Henry, in his commentary on Jeremiah 5:21, wrote, "None so blind as those that will not see." Jesus said, "Blessed are the pure in heart; for they shall see God." (Matthew 5:8) Not with physical but with spiritual eyes, of course. Those of us who seek purity in our hearts can begin to know and understand the God Principle at work in our lives and in the world around us. We can see and feel God in action and actively seek to live so as to fit into His plans. See what I mean?

PARABLE OF THE
SUPER -HEROES

Y ou never know where ideas are going to come from when you're a writer. Some mornings an idea is perched on my head like a pet parakeet waiting for me to wake up and feed it. Other times a good idea plays hide and seek and has to be coaxed from its secret place before it can be tamed.

Today was a hide and seek day. I checked out all the usual places...e-mail, news headlines, Facebook items, etc. Nope. "It" wasn't there.

The next step was to go to my collection of Parables Notes...some of which have been gathering dust—or, perhaps I should think of them as ripening—for as much as ten years of more. And there it was. "*Parable of The* Pitchfork" had been patiently waiting to be found in this little idea game since passed to me by my friend Wanda Cooley in 2007.

Wanda told about a well-used pitchfork that had been left behind when workmen delivered a truck-load of mulch to her garden plot...probably left because it had outlived its usefulness. It didn't look like much. The snaggle-toothed tines were bent out of line. The handle had been worn down so it was several inches shorter than it used to be; and it had been left out in the weather so often that it was almost like a piece of driftwood, and too light for their purpose.

That handicapped pitchfork, with all its apparent problems, found a welcome foster-home in Wanda's toolshed. She found the misaligned tines perfect for weeding...the wizened handle was the ideal length and weight for her use. What had been discarded as beyond its usefulness suited her purposes exactly.

You will no doubt have noticed that this isn't the *Parable of The* Pitchfork. That's because, although Wanda's experience was the inspiration, my train of thought quickly left that stop and moved on to another station.

Although you may not be old enough to have been a fan of Marvel Comics with its stable of Super Heroes, you have probably at least heard of the X-Men series of movies that have been so popular the last ten years of so. The X-Men (or should we refer to them as the X-Persons?) were a group of young men and women called Mutants who demonstrated "special powers due to their possession of the 'X-Gene,' a gene which normal humans lack and which gives Mutants their abilities. Early on, however, the 'X' in X-Men stood for 'extra' power which normal humans lacked. Also alluded to was that mutations occurred as a result of radiation exposure." (Wikipedia)

The basic premise of the comic book series was that these mutants didn't fit into normal society because of their special "gifts," and were increasingly ostracized. Under this cloud of increasing anti-mutant sentiment, "Professor Xavier created a haven at his Westchester mansion to train young mutants to use their powers for the benefit of humanity, and to prove mutants can be heroes." (Thanks again, Wikipedia.)

Have you ever considered the thought that each of us could be thought of as X-Men? You have to agree that we each have talents, skills and abilities that set us apart from those around us. Maybe not *super* powers, but certainly separate and special powers. Many who fail to appreciate the source and purpose of those gifts might even consider us different, or strange, because of them.

The singer and actress Ethel Waters is quoted as saying "God don't make no junk." I agree with her, and I firmly believe that every one of our powers is special and intended by the Creator to be used by us to bless and benefit those around us.

You and I are unique, though we may not fulfill someone else's idea of what is attractive or useful, and if we are trying to fit in with the Lord's plan, we really are Super Heroes. We have a special purpose in this life and a special place awaiting us in His Kingdom. So...Up, up and away!

PARABLE OF THE SHELL SEEKERS

T he scene was familiar. I've been there many times over the forty-five years or so since we first were introduced to Pawleys Island, South Carolina. I've traced those sands before dawn, after dark and in the heat of day...alone and in the company of friends, children and grandchildren.

The silence of a solitary walk is what I prize the most...but a purposeful stroll with companions of any age runs a close second. The commanding, rhythmic spilling of the day's delivery of tidal waves always has the effect of making me talk more softly for some reason... or maybe it just seems that way...almost as if I was talking in church, not wanting to disturb others.

My walks on the beach usually start out the same way, with me striding purposefully along...a distance power walker with someplace to go. As I reach the end of my imaginary tether, when it's time to turn around and head back, my pace becomes more studied, my concentration more specific, as I begin to pay more attention to the shells and miscellaneous flotsam and jetsam deposited and uncovered by the flowing waters.

Each year...and, I suppose each season...there seems to be a tendency to have one or two "specials." You know what I mean...one time it'll be an abundance of sand dollars, another time it's sea pens, or angel wings, or keyhole limpets, or lady-slippers. One year there seemed to be the shells of calico crabs everywhere. This year the special was starfish. I don't know when I've ever seen so many starfish brought in by the surf at Pawleys.

This year I was moved to consider how our tastes and interests change with the passing of the years. It was made clear to me as I watched my grandchildren while they inspected and selected from the daily array of treasures spread on the sand with all the random organization of articles arrayed at a yard sale.

As I studied some of the "beach booty" gleaned from the ocean's offerings, I asked our little Anna the same question I have asked her siblings...and her mother and aunts on similar visits in years long gone by. "Why did you want to keep that?", indicating some broken piece, or shard of sea debris.

She gave me the same answer I've heard so many times before: "Because I thought it was pretty." I've been asked that same question... and answered with the same response.

At this time of my life, I don't usually bother with anything but whole, perfect or near-perfect shells. And not just *any* shells, either... usually specific shells, depending upon the seasonal offerings. True, the pretty shells and fragments do attract my attention, but I don't give them much time or effort. After all, I've collected my share of flotsam just because it was "pretty."

But, wait a minute! Don't be so quick to dismiss those broken, imperfect and unattractive bits and pieces of shells...those sea pebbles in the surf...those washed-up stems of seaweed. Sure, they don't look like much now...they may not appear beautiful or useful now...but, when studied with the unbiased eye of a child, they still inspire awe and wonder.

Whatever a shell seeker is looking for, whether it's color, shape or texture...whether it is perfect outline or surface...it is always good to remember that there's not a single particle or fragment to be discovered that has no appeal to the discerning eye. Isn't it a little presumptuous for us to judge anything created by the Hand of God to be ugly or useless?

When the Lord inspects His creation, He doesn't see us as we see ourselves...broken, imperfect and unattractive. He sees the beauty and utility He designed in each of us, and is ready to help us live up to His expectations. Unlike those shells and fragments, however, we get to make the choice of whether or not to surrender to His Hand.

I value...no, treasure...those bits and pieces of beach stuff offered to me by my little shell seekers just because they thought they were pretty. Just as surely, our Lord treasures each life offering we bring to Him, and accepts us as worthy and beautiful.

Jesus challenged His disciples to be fishers of men. It isn't too far-fetched to imagine Him admonishing us to be shell-seekers of men... looking for inner beauty and potential in every person with whom we come into contact...bringing them back to Him for His approval, and hearing Him say, "Well done, thou good and faithful shell-seeker."

PARABLE OF THE CONDITIONAL RESPONSE

In this age of the digital substitute for personal communication, I doubt there's anyone who hasn't received through their Inbox at least a few of those interesting pictures with humorous and sometimes hilarious captions. Someone, somewhere, expends an amazing amount of time and effort to accumulate, create and disseminate these witty commentaries. Not to mention the total time frittered away by the recipients who read, respond and forward them.

In fact, you've probably received an e-mail, a YouTube link, or a Facebook or Twitter post showing a series of photographs of dogs of all shapes, breeds and sizes, each accompanied by a fitting tag line. I received one like that the other day, and I confess that I fell into the cuteness trap and spent five or ten minutes scrolling through them. (Don't raise your eyebrows at me..."Let him who is without sin..." All right, probably more than ten minutes, but that's not my point.)

One photo in particular that came to mind today was of an adorable Dachshund puppy, looking earnestly into the camera above the caption, "Thank goodness you're here! Someone has pooped on the hall carpet!"

It just happened that the same thing happened a few days ago with my mostly Black Lab, Suzy Q. She had nudged my elbow for attention several times, then gave up and left the study where I was working. An hour or so later I walked down the hall and found...well, need I continue? Placed there, more or less neatly...one of those "Well, I tried to tell you" messages piled on the carpet.

Carefully disguising my voice and adopting the tone of praise and affection I asked, "What do we have here? Did you leave this special gift for me?" Affecting childlike innocence, avoiding eye contact and looking for spiderwebs in the corner of the ceiling, Suzy acted as if she hadn't heard my question...or hoped that I would find someone else to blame for this disgraceful act.

Whether Suzy had a guilty conscience or not doesn't really matter, does it? As I cleaned up the mess, I thought about what I could do to keep this from happening again. Animal experts tell us that scolding and punishment aren't effective unless the pet has been caught in the act, so there aren't many options.

When Suzy Q commits one of those acts of animal indulgence... gnawing household goods, soiling the carpets, devouring forbidden fruits and other edible objects...I forgive her. Then I can either physically restrain her or move those temptations out of her reach.

That may be all right for animals, but what about relationships between humans? What kind of commitment should be required before we render forgiveness for an offense? In most human relationships forgiveness is conditional. It is generally expected that one must confess and repent...change one's ways and in some cases make restitution...in order to earn the forgiveness of the one who was offended.

In Psalm 32, David describes the torment and anguish suffered by a guilty party...torture that was only relieved when that guilt was confessed and repentance was begun. He contrasts that with the unequaled joy that results when the transgression has been forgiven and the record wiped clean.

In some ways, the manner in which humans deal with each other and the way God deals with mankind are alike. In both cases forgiveness is unavailable to the wrongdoer until the wrong has been confessed. However, among men a restoration to good standing depends upon good behavior.

With God, when confession is genuine and repentance is sincere, there are no conditions. Forgiveness is instantaneous and complete. The penalty for guilt is completely removed.

When Suzy Q commits the sin of emission on the carpet, I have no choice but to clean it up. Notice that Scripture doesn't imply that the scars and debris of our misdeeds are taken away. They remain as a reminder of our sin...a caution as well as an encouragement to others who are tempted in the same way.

Finally, unlike our dealings with pets, where we must constantly attempt to train them not to do those things that displease us, our God has the patience to treat us differently. In verse 8 of David's Psalm, we read "I will instruct you and teach you in the way you should go; I will guide you with my eye." (NKJV) If we will simply pay attention, He will keep us from committing those same transgressions again. No wonder he says the upright in heart can shout for joy.

So, the progression is confession, repentance, forgiveness, release and joy. That's why I like the way Eugene Peterson interpreted verse eleven in his *The Message, the Bible in Contemporary Language,* "Celebrate God. Sing together—everyone! All your honest hearts, raise the roof!"

That gives a whole new meaning to the expression "Confession is good for the soul," doesn't it? Are you ready to go out and raise the roof?

PARABLE OF THE SECOND MILE

The internet is a marvelous technological development. The degree of marvel it generates varies, of course, with the generation of the user. For every internet aficionado who swears by it, there are many computer curmudgeons who regularly swear *at* it. But, love it or hate it, there's no denying that, with patience and effort, even the least enthusiastic visitor to the wonderful world-wide web can glean occasional nuggets of value from the information stream.

Considering my generation, I'm only moderately mystified by the magical methods of on-line meandering, and can even find what I happen to be looking for...much of the time. To tell the truth, though, a great deal of the information I pick up from the internet comes to me involuntarily, through forwarded e-mails, from newsletters and web page updates I didn't know I was signed up for, etc. Some I keep, some I pass on and some I dispense with a touch of the deadly Delete key.

For several years I received The Word of the Day, sent out by Merriam-Webster's on-line dictionary. I learned a lot of new words, as well as the definitions and origins of words that were uncommon or less familiar.

One of the new favorite words I learned was *lagniappe*, pronounced lahn-YOPP. Lagniappe is a noun and comes from two words that literally translate *the something added*. It is "something given or obtained gratuitously or by way of good measure," and is most commonly used to designate some small gift given a customer by a merchant at the time of a purchase. (Think "baker's dozen" where one pays for a dozen and receives thirteen, and you'll have the idea.)

Lagniappe is something extra thrown in as a bonus. Not like a Tip, which is presumably extra payment for services rendered in a pleasing or efficient manner, and is paid by the customer.

As I considered the concept of lagniappe, the something added, if occurred to me that the concept isn't new at all. In fact, it is reflected in numerous teachings in the Bible, with probably the most familiar appearing in the Sermon on the Mount. In Matthew 5:39-41, Jesus told the disciples, "But I tell you, do not resist an evil person. If someone strikes you on the right cheek, turn to him the other also. And if someone wants to sue you and take your tunic, let him have your cloak as well. If someone forces you to go one mile, go with him two miles. Give to the one who asks you, and do not turn away from the one who wants to borrow from you." (NIV)

I think that is the essence of lagniappe. Think about it. Someone strikes you because he has a grievance...believes he has a right to. Jesus says we should give him the something added, another shot. (Of course, there is the little boy who added his own interpretation of the verse and said, "The Bible didn't say what to do if he hits the other cheek, so I lit in and beat the daylights out of him.") If someone wins a lawsuit and takes your jacket, give him your topcoat, too... the something added.

Verse forty-one is perhaps the most quoted...and, misapplied... verse in this section. Jesus referred to a Roman law requiring Jewish citizens to carry a Roman soldier's burden for no less than one mile when ordered to do so. He told his disciples that in addition to the first mile they should give the lagniappe, the something added, and carry the burden a second mile.

Here's why I believe that this concept of "going the second mile" is so often applied incorrectly: There's a certain amount of glory and pride that attaches to going the second mile, but the first mile is considered nothing more than drudgery, and consequently something to be endured, tolerated...and that often with obvious ill-will.

One of my dad's favorite and most often-repeated quotes was one by Elbert Hubbard: "Folks who never do any more than they are paid for, never get paid for any more than they do." That's quite true. But listen, my friend, there's no blessing in going the *second* mile, if you begrudge the first one. Often in life it is one's second effort that makes the difference between success and failure. But without the completion of a first effort there can never *be* a second.

Grace is God's lagniappe, giving us more than we deserve, more than we could ever hope to pay for. Jesus endured the first mile so God could give the something added, the second mile.

Today's not too soon to give someone lagniappe...go the second mile. How about it? Now's the time to give it a try, don't you think?

PARABLE OF THE DARK GLASS

I finally gave in and got some new glasses the other day. The old ones didn't seem to do the job anymore. After a few years they just appeared to lose their strength. Maybe the lenses got worn out, or something…I haven't figured it out yet. Anyway, the new ones work fine.

This time I got some of those lenses that get darker in the sunlight. I've had them before, but the last time the glass lenses were so heavy they were uncomfortable. I like the much lighter acrylic lenses better.

I tested my glasses like a child plays with a new toy…stepping into the sunlight and back into the shade…to see how long it took for the change to take place. I figure it takes about as long as it would for me to remember where my sunglasses are, go get them and put them on. And I think they just look cool.

I've thought a lot recently about how much time and technology have been devoted to the study of how to get protection from the effects of exposure to the sun. Not only from the light itself, but from the heat and the ultra-violet rays the sun generates.

Truly, we have also developed a large number of products and processes to harness the energy of the sun's rays. We now have solar panels that can convert sunlight into electrical energy to operate devices of all shapes and sizes, from cell phones and pocket calculators to entire space stations orbiting the earth.

Add to that panels designed to collect and store heat for warming water and to reduce the expense of keeping homes and buildings comfortably warm in even the harshest weather. Indeed, we have come a long way towards applying this boundless, free resource to make our lives a little easier and more satisfying.

However, as persistent as scientists have been in learning to harness the sun's energy for the benefit of mankind, I'm sure that most of us are much more aware of efforts that have been directed toward protecting us from that same sun's powerful rays.

Mothers have been conditioned to be sure their children have put on their sun-screen lotions and ointments before going out to play. (After all, when you get to be as old as I am, you don't want to have skin that looks like leather, do you?) I have a wide-brimmed "fishing hat" that is supposed to provide protection up to 51 SPF...whatever that may mean. Recently I saw swim shirts designed for surfers, that offered superior protection from the sun. All this to protect us from the serious threat of deadly skin cancers resulting from too much sun exposure.

Whenever there is a report of a total or partial solar eclipse, there are multiple warnings concerning how to safely observe it. We all know by now that we cannot look directly at the sun without damaging our eyes. It can only be viewed through special glasses such as welders use, or specially prepared film that only admits a small amount of the light.

The Bible makes several references to God appearing as a bright light, causing men to hide their eyes. Just as a kitchen light turned on in the middle of the night sends insects and other unwanted creatures scuttling for the shadows, the pure light of God's presence makes sinful man want to withdraw to dark places of comfort and security. God doesn't hide Himself from us because He desires privacy, or wants to "keep us in the dark." He does it for our protection.

When Paul talks with the believers in Corinth about perfect love, he talks about the time "when that which is perfect is come" …when we will no longer "know in part"…no longer "see through a glass darkly." In that day all believers will be able to rejoice in the Heavenly Sunlight…the light of Bright Heaven's Son…without Son screen, Son glasses or Son shades.

PARABLE OF THE FLASHLIGHT

For a number of years my wife, Lyn, and I had a fun way to celebrate birthdays. She got the idea from one of the folks she worked with...and after more than four decades of trying to think of ways to make the days more enjoyable it was refreshing.

Instead of trying to come up with one big knockout gift, we agreed to the plan of giving a more modest gift each day for the entire week before the appointed day. The usual rules for spousal "gifting" ...for my gifts to her that mainly meant nothing with a cord attached... were suspended, and practical gifts were allowed.

One such birth week benevolence from me was a small rechargeable emergency flashlight. It plugs into a wall socket, constantly recharging until the power goes off, or until otherwise needed. That was one of those practical gifts that was really appreciated. We both used it a lot.

That flashlight's usefulness has increased considerably in the last few months, since Suzy Q...like a four-legged Mary Poppins summoned to set in order all things domestic...came to our house to stay. Now the light gets a regular workout.

Because of my current schedule many of my daily household chores run into the evening, so that our usual final patrol of the day often occurs as the day's light is waning. Often, it's well after dark before we can begin our trek.

That's when I reach for the handy flashlight. Not because I can't make my way around the neighborhood in the darkness, or to protect myself from strangers lurking in the shadows. But for a rather more practical reason than those, as reasonable as they may be.

One of the purposes of these excursions in the dark and semi-dark is so that Suzy Q can have the final one of what my grandmother used to call her "daily constitutionals." This is especially important if she hasn't made her afternoon treasure deposit.

Some years ago, when I walked our mostly English Setter Cody in the neighborhood, it was considered normal, and for the most part acceptable, to simply leave those deposits where they occurred. Nowadays most folks agree that was rude, crude and unsanitary behavior...so anyone with any sense of what is good and proper is equipped with a supply of "pooper bags" so they can whisk away those unwelcome presents. (The grandchildren view this operation with perverse delight. "Ewwww...you touched poop...can I do it next time?")

So that's why, when we gird up our loins to do the day's last duty, I reach for the ever-handy flashlight. When it's dark you don't want to just go groping around on the ground for that kind of stuff, you know.

Here's something to think about. Just what is a flashlight...or any lamp, chandelier or candle, for that matter...useful for, anyway?

To begin with, it lets passersby know that you're there. When you're walking it lets motorists avoid you. When you're at home, lights make the house look appealing and comfortable.

Whether in the house or out in the world, a flashlight, lamp or candle reveals things not visible in the darkness and shadows. It can eliminate the mystery, fear and danger of things unseen, and help us to avoid obstacles that can harm and delay us.

Don't you think these are some of the things Jesus had in His mind when He declared Believers to be the light of the world? He was directing us to be like flashlights in a dark world, easily identified in that darkness, attractive and welcoming...offering comfort and hope.

The light of our lives should help identify the filth and evil lurking in that darkness, show the way to avoid the obstacles placed in our paths by the adversary and his minions. And once the wickedness and obstacles have been recognized, our light should encourage and make possible their clean up and removal.

Finally, our light should be used to lead the way to and along the difficult and narrow Path marked out by Jesus in His loving instructions. We are told to put into action His Word, which, as the Psalmist said, "...is a lamp unto my feet and a light unto my path."

Pray that the Lord will help you keep your flashlight charged and ready to shine.

PARABLE OF THE GATE

There is a recent TV show that seems to be popular, at least this week. The way these shows come and go it may not be around by the time my printer finishes with this page, but at least it appears to be doing well for the present. It's called The Gates.

From the promotion for The Gates, I gather it's about the current fad of vampires and werewolves. It features a cast of attractive young actors and deals with their trials and tribulations as they try to get along in a modern gated community, and a world that simply doesn't understand them. I suppose it's not easy being occasionally covered in fur, with blood dripping from your chin. As if being a young person these days wasn't bad enough.

Personally, I haven't had much interest in the lifestyles of the furry and bloodthirsty since the days of Bela Lugosi, Lon Chaney and "Abbott and Costello Meet the Wolfman." I have to admit that I have no idea why there's this fascination with this particular segment of the supernatural. Maybe it's just the result of boredom with the flood of shows about crime, espionage and doctors. Maybe it's those attractive young actors. I couldn't tell you.

In fact, I am so disconnected from the vampire thing that almost every time I see a promotion for "The Gates," my mind goes in a completely different direction. Would you believe that the mention of Gates makes me think of the Bible?

Remember the verse in Matthew 16:18 that says "...I will build My church, and the gates of hell shall not prevail against it"? Ever wonder why there are gates in hell? What is the purpose of gates...and why, of all places, does hell have a need for them?

In the days when the Lord spoke those words to Peter and the disciples, gates were understood to have a specific purpose. Just as they have today.

Some gates are intended to keep out unwanted intruders...wild animals...marauders...unwelcome visitors. Other gates are designed to keep things inside the walls safe and secure. Still others have the purpose of keeping people or other creatures separated from those they might harm, as in the gates of a jail or prison...or a cage at the zoo.

In ancient times, the prosperity and power of a city were judged by the quality of its gates...both the materials from which they were made and the number and placement of them. The same could be said then, as now, for the gates before an estate or community.

But *hell*? Who would want to get into hell? Christians aren't going there. And as for getting out...well, those souls consigned there will have no power to escape, regardless of gates. So, what could Jesus possibly mean when He says the gates of hell shall not hold up against an assault by the Church? Just what are those gates designed for, anyway?

Well...here's the way I see it, in case you'd like to know a layman's opinion.

I don't believe that Jesus was speaking about the eternal afterlife when He addressed the subject of the faith of His disciples. His concern was how they were to conduct their lives and their witness to the people of their day...and the example that would provide for us today.

The Lord was referring to the artificial spiritual barriers the adversary has convinced us exist, separating souls he has laid claim to from any hope of redemption. When we talk about the multitudes of addictions that have been "discovered" and identified in recent years... so-called diseases that explain why individuals resort to self-destructive and un- or anti-social behavior...we're really talking about gates, aren't we? Gates that hold soul's captive and cut them off from any hope of receiving help from those on the "outside"? Could those be the gates of hell?

If, for just a moment, we think of these propensities, these desires, these addictions as the gates Jesus were referring to, think what that means to us as Believers. He made the unqualified assertion that those gates cannot hold up against any assault by the Church. The Church? That's you and me, folks...*we're* the Church!

Our dominance over those gates has several implications, but there are two that are of particular importance to me...and should be to you as well. First, the gates set up by the adversary cannot confine us against our will. Our overriding faith in Jesus as Lord will give us the power to break through the gates of any addiction or weakness whenever we choose.

Secondly, those gates cannot prevent us from reaching the unsaved with the message of salvation on any occasion when we make a determined assault. That doesn't guarantee that the lost ones will choose to escape that bondage, but that will be a choice they must make. We don't have the power...any more than God Himself has... to make them believe. He relinquished that power the moment He granted mankind freedom of will.

It is not for us, the Church, to weigh the cost of assaulting these gates of hell against the bare possibility that some souls may or may not be liberated. Our success is not measured in such quantitative

terms. Our success is counted in terms of only one thing: the fact that we showed up for the assault. The simple state of being prepared and determined to heed the command to "CHARGE!" is what God values and rewards.

I hope this idea of God's open gate policy encourages you to try rattling some of those gate latches that have kept you in...or out...in the past. I know it has done that for me.

PARABLE OF THE CHRISTMAS PARABLE

The other day someone asked me if I had written a Christmas parable. I had to stop and think for a minute before I remembered the Parable of The Jolly Holiday, which was mostly concerned with the sometimes-heated discussions between those who celebrate the season as a Christian holiday and those who prefer to think of it as a secular holiday.

As I sit and think about those things which make Christmas a truly meaningful holiday...things which have not been the object of countless seasonal sermons and lessons...several images came to mind. Most of them recognizable the world over as signs of the annual holiday.

I saw bearded men in red suits...some seated in shopping malls, with wriggling children on their laps, others standing beside small caldrons, ringing bells to attract generous givers. There are images of frolicking snowmen with top hats, leading troops of happy children.

Projected on the screen inside my forehead there are pictures of that grotesque green furry creature with a heart that's too small. Don't forget the scraggly shrub that is transformed into a beautiful tree when lovingly decorated by little round-headed children. And a sad little reindeer with a peculiar proboscis, finding his calling as a guiding light.

100

By the way, I learned last night that there are three previously unknown reindeer...aside from Rudolph...that have recently been discovered. Olive, Annie and Waldo. They're in that song about Rudolph, you know. "Olive, the other reindeer, used to laugh and call him names. They wouldn't let poor Rudolph play in Annie Reindeer's games." And, "Now Waldo Reindeer loves him..." Bet you didn't know about them, did you? But I digress.

Blaring TV commercials brashly vie for the attention of viewers and their dollars. The silver bells clang incessantly. The internet is deluged by a tsunami of images of houses, lawns and shops that make the Griswald's Family Christmas look like a kindergarten exercise. The bigger, louder and more garish the better. "Come on! Get in the Christmas spirit!" they urge.

Don't misunderstand me. I think the joy and abandon of an outrageous celebration can be a good thing in itself. Good for the mind and good for the spirit. But Christians have fallen too much into the spell of the World to the extent that we have tended to give the impression that the joyous greetings and extravagant gifts are what the season is all about. And it most certainly is not.

In order to understand as Believers our true responsibility to share the reason for the joy that is in us, and to portray the real meaning behind our celebration, let me suggest an example. Suppose you found yourself leaving your physician's office having just received the news that you had an incurable form of cancer. Incurable. No chance of escape. Only a few weeks of life remaining.

You go through days and weeks of dread and despair. Nothing can bring you joy.

Then, one evening you receive a call from your doctor with the news, "We have discovered a cure for your cancer. Come in tomorrow and we will begin treatment. You'll see improvement immediately. Your life has been saved."

How do you think you'd feel? Would you celebrate? Would you want to tell everyone you meet about the miraculous cure available to all who have that disease? Would you begin to live your life differently?

Now, here's the million-dollar question: would you get angry and argue with those who didn't believe your story...who refused to seek the treatment for their cancer?

The World has been diagnosed with the fatal disease of sin. The penalty for that sin is eternal death. God has devised a cure for sin... relief from our death penalty. That cure came to earth as a little baby... fully God, fully Man. This birth is what we celebrate at Christmas.

Celebrate the season in such a way that each person you meet will want to seek the cure you've found.

PARABLE OF THE GOOD SCOUT

I've forgotten where I saw this, but the scene was of a man who was supposed to make some sort of speech when the unthinkable happened...the sort of thing that many people fear when asked to speak in public...his mind went blank. He couldn't even begin to think of what he had planned to say. In his panic his brain kicked into emergency mode and he began to recite the first thing that came into his mind.

"On my honor, I will do my best...To do my duty to God and my country and to obey the Scout Law...To help other people at all times...To keep myself physically strong, mentally awake and morally straight." I didn't have to stop for a second to recall those words...I had learned them, too, as a boy...the familiar words of the Boy Scout Oath.

Isn't it funny the things we remember in a crisis? The only thing he didn't add was the Boy Scout Motto: "Be Prepared." Oh, and the words of the Scout Law, which assert that a Scout is "Trustworthy, Loyal, Helpful..." etc. I also learned all those high ideals during the short time I was a Boy Scout. I admit that I wasn't much of a scout overall, but I at least learned the book part.

I think I must have written at some time about the depth of my commitment to the experience of Scouting. The best example I can think of was when I was trying to earn my Tenderfoot badge...the very first accomplishment for a new Scout. We were supposed to cook a meal over a campfire. I brought a can of Campbell's Soup...without a can opener.

All right...laugh if you wish, but ask yourself, "What are the first things to fly off the shelves at the super market when a disaster is expected? Milk, bread and *canned goods*, right? Do you go out and shoot a few squirrels and gather sticks and twigs for firewood? I think not!

"Be Prepared" means different things to different people, after all. Anyway, shortly after that episode, the family moved back to Atlanta and I never got back into Scouting. I always remembered the Oath, the Law and the Motto, though.

These thoughts all came to mind a few days ago while I was at the memorial service for a friend who had graduated into the Kingdom. The son and a grandson of this wonderful Christian gentleman each got up to share some of their cherished memories of him and recount examples of his philosophy of life and living.

One remarkable habit of his was that of riding his bicycle to work almost every day of his thirty-year career as an aeronautical engineer with Lockheed Martin. When asked if he rode it when there was bad weather, he responded, "There's no such thing as bad weather...there are only unprepared people."

I've thought about that statement a lot of times the last few days, and, you know, he's right. Weather is weather...whether we approve of it or not makes no difference. There is no good...or bad...weather. The thing that qualifies it as good or bad in our minds is the degree to which we are prepared for it...a purely human factor.

As Will Rogers said, "Everybody complains about the weather, but nobody does anything about it." Before you say there's nothing we can do about the weather, just remember we can be prepared to deal with whatever weather occurs.

How well are you prepared to weather the storms of life? Jesus told his disciples that the wise man builds his house on a firm

foundation so it will be prepared to withstand the storms that will surely come. His entire ministry was focused on teaching them how to prepare themselves and others. And, I promise you, the Boy Scout Handbook can't touch the Bible as a resource to help us be prepared... and to "present us faultless before the presence of His glory with exceeding joy."

PARABLE OF THE DAILY DOSE

I began this morning's writing session as I usually do, standing or sitting as I take the first sips of what one of my best friends calls my "dose" of morning coffee. He said that he never really liked coffee all that much, but that his body didn't seem to cooperate very well first thing in the morning until he provided it with its daily dose of the "mystic medication."

So...as I thoughtfully sipped my daily dose of coffee, I waited expectantly to be "inspirated" with the subject for today's writing. With my imaginary remote control, I began to click through brain channels...scanning articles and news items of the last few days. Finally, I felt that gentle, mental nudge when I came to one about George Beverly Shea.

Bev—I can't imagine anyone who has ever heard this beloved singer of hymns of the Faith who didn't immediately feel like he was a personal friend you could call by his nickname—is currently celebrating his one hundred and third birthday. That's right. He's 103...and still singing.

I've written about waking up as a small boy and hearing the radio playing in Dad's room as he got ready for work. In those days, the morning broadcasts from WSB, the South's premier clear-channel radio station, consisted of Southern gospel, bluegrass, farmers' news... and the singing of George Beverly Shea, years before he became the musical voice of the Billy Graham Crusades.

I can hear his golden bass echoing in the studio in the back of my head..."Singing I go, along life's road; Praising the Lord, Praising the Lord...for Jesus has lifted my load." I remember reading that his mother would waken his family many mornings, playing and singing that song.

To this day there are multitudes of songs on my list of favorites that I can only imagine in the voice of Bev Shea. "I'd Rather Have Jesus" and "How Great Thou Art," of course...and "The Old Rugged Cross," "When They Ring Those Golden Bells," and...well, you get the idea.

Recently, at one of the assisted living facilities where we conduct services, after leading in the singing of a few hymns and singing a solo of personal testimony, I sat listening to the message delivered by my associate pastor. As he spoke, I heard Bev begin to sing softly...'way back in my mental studio...a musical accompaniment to the spoken words. The lyrics of the song were an excellent paring with the point of the lesson, and when he was finished, I was moved to sing...

"Day by day, and with each passing moment,
Strength, I find to meet my trials here.
Trusting in my father's wise bestowment,
I've no cause for worry or for fear.
He whose heart is kind beyond all measure
Gives unto each day what He deems best—
Lovingly, it's part of pain and pleasure,
Mingling toil with peace and rest."

The hymn is titled "Day by Day." Ahhh...that's the secret, isn't it? A daily dose of the Lord's strength, trust, faith, kindness, love, peace and rest. Administered each and every day, like manna in the desert, sufficient for each day's needs with nothing left over, except what we need to share with all those around us.

Without the dispensation of that daily dose of love and care, even the strongest and heartiest of Believers would suffer spiritual malnutrition. That is the supplement that provides the strength and courage to be witnesses, even when things seem to go wrong.

This daily dose is so essential for the full and meaningful life the Lord intended for us that He gladly and consistently provides free samples to any who will receive them. Haven't you ever wondered how even people as mean as snakes occasionally have a sense of peace and comfort? That's simply a free sample of the Lord's Daily Dose.

He's so eager for you to experience His love and peace that he licensed me and a multitude of others to help dispense those doses. If you haven't had yours today, we are commissioned to provide one to you.

PARABLE OF THE PLACE TO GO

"**S**on, walk like you have someplace to go."

If you have read many of these parables, you are already aware of the good relationship I had with my father, and have probably discerned the great respect I had...and have...for his words of wisdom. That has continued, even though I have since learned that much of his wisdom was of the "do as I say, not as I do" variety—just as it is with most human fathers.

It won't come as a surprise, then, that when he saw me poking along on some unwilling errand, he uttered that stern quotation above. He told me time and again not to amble, stroll, mosey, meander or wander...but to walk with a purpose. Walk as if you're on an important mission...even when you're not. It'll impress some, mystify some, and fool quite a few who put a greater value on appearances than on results.

In an early scene from Meredith Wilson's musical hit "The Music Man," Marian the Librarian, while in a discussion with her mother, hears her piano student begin to lag as she picks out a lesson on the keyboard. "Don't dawdle, Amaryllis," she calls. Don't dawdle. That's my message in a nutshell. Get going; keep on going; get the job done.

That advice is not to be confused with the humorous suggestion I came across a while back that recommended "When you feel like walking around, walk briskly and carry some papers or perhaps a file folder in one hand. People will think you're on an important errand and won't interrupt you."

Walking as if you had a place to go has many benefits, in addition to the obvious one that you'll reach your destination more quickly. Fitness experts have told us for years that purposeful walking is one of the best forms of aerobic exercise. It is great for the cardio-vascular system and burns almost as many calories as jogging...without all the damage to the feet and knees.

A steadfast stride can also have powerful psychological results. In much the same way that "whistling a happy tune" can trick the brain into a happier attitude, an energetic walk can make even a tiresome journey or an unpleasant destination less distasteful.

In these modern times, walking isn't very highly regarded—outside the circles of those intent upon physical fitness, of course. I've seen folks hop in the car to go down the driveway and pick up their mail. Golfers, supposedly on the course for the exercise and fresh air, motor around the grounds on golf carts. Trams carry travelers from the parking lots to the arenas and air terminals. Even grocery stores have motorized shopping carts for the disabled...used by some who are just unwilling to walk. Walking anywhere has come to be noteworthy. Too bad.

In many years of Bible study in preparation for teaching Sunday School, I learned that in the New Testament the Greek word most often translated "walk" is the word *peripateo* (pronounced *peh-ree-pah-teh'-o*). Literally, it means to tread all around; to live, deport oneself; to be occupied with; to walk around, as a sentry on duty walks his post.

Simply put, our walk—our way of living—as Christians should be carried out as those who, indeed, have some place to go...a place worth going to...a place worth the journey...a place to look forward to. And isn't that true for us, of all people? After all, we're bound for the Promised Land!

So, here's my word for you, straight from God's Word: Walk with enthusiasm, walk with joy in your heart and a bounce in your step. Especially when you don't *feel* very joyful or bouncy. Climb those stairs two at a time as long as you're physically able. Set a good example for how to conduct the Christian walk.

Do you remember the character Igor in the old black and white movies? He would tell the visitors "Walk this way," as he ambled off with his hunchback gait. Since that early film, comedy sketches have parodied that scene, with the visitors attempting to match that angular, shuffling gait. Your responsibility as a Christian witness is to show those observing you how to conduct the Christian walk and how to walk His way.

Encourage those whose steps may be faltering. Bring them along with you...with your arms around them, or carried on your shoulders if necessary. None need be aimless or homeless...we all have a place to go. A destination well worthy of our best efforts.

Don't dawdle...don't mosey. For where you're going there are folks, you're eager to see...folks who are eagerly awaiting your arrival. Jesus and heaven's angels are cheering you on as you keep on the course for the Kingdom. Pace on with patience and persistence.

So, conduct your daily walk like you have someplace to go... as indeed you do, if you're a Believer. And be sure that your walk demonstrates your determination to arrive at that divine destination. I guarantee you that you'll enjoy the trip a lot more, and you'll be a great inspiration for others as they toil along. Besides that, you'll reach that precious place before you know it.

PARABLE OF THE AUTOMATIC CHOKE

S ome of my fondest memories from early childhood have to do with riding with Mom and Dad in our pre-World War II Chevrolet. If I remember correctly, it had a windshield that you could crank out a few inches at the bottom for extra ventilation. And those window vents that you could open all the way forward to scoop in more air for a cooling breeze. That was the latest thing in air conditioning in those days, let me tell you.

I recall many times when Dad would hoist me into his lap so that I could "drive," anxiously jerking the wheel from side to side as I tried to keep the car on the road. It never occurred to me that he had his fingers on the wheel, just in case.

Another thing about that old Chevy that I remember is that it had a manual choke. Most folks under 60 probably don't know what that is, I suppose. Whenever it was time to start the car...especially in cold weather...the driver had to pull out the knob labeled "Choke" to allow the right amount of gas into the carburetor to get the cold engine to crank.

That extra bit of gas was critical for starting, but as the engine got warmed up it used too much gas, so the choke knob had to be pushed back in. Proper use of the choke had to be learned. Pull it out too far and too much gas would flood into the carburetor...not far enough and the engine wouldn't get enough fuel for it to start. If the engine got "flooded," it took five minutes or so for the gas to evaporate so the driver could try again.

If you have a gas-powered lawnmower, string-trimmer, leaf blower or other tool of that sort, you know about choking and flooding. Choking and flooding have led many otherwise genteel and cultured people to resort to words that are swearable.

I remember as a young person watching a TV program called Mister Wizard, where the kindly, white-headed neighbor would welcome a couple of youngsters into his workshop and would explain and demonstrate a wide variety of scientific principles. On one show he gave the perfect explanation for what causes flooding in an internal combustion engine.

He took an eye-dropper of gasoline and put it into an open bowl and lit it with a match. Of course, you know what happened. Whoosh! It lit and burned for a second or two.

Next, Mister Wizard poured about a cup of gasoline into a specially-made clear cylinder. (Hey, kids! Don't try this at home!) Then he lowered a wire with a sparkplug attached into the gas so that it was completely covered. When he put electricity to the plug, you could see the spark under the surface of the gasoline, but nothing happened!

He then explained to the youngsters the prime principle of combustion. In order for combustion to take place there must be the correct amount of two elements: 1) Combustible material and 2) Oxygen. Too much or too little of either one will interfere with combustion.

However, at least in the area of the modern automobile, the Automatic...and, nowadays, computerized...Choke has changed that. As much of a pain as they are for those who like to tinker with automobiles, the introduction of on-board computers that monitor conditions for combustion eliminates the likelihood that an engine will flood if all is properly adjusted.

Have you ever stopped to think how similar those gasoline engines are to humans? We are cautioned our entire lives to observe moderation in all things. The reason is that when we indulge in too much of anything...no matter how good and beneficial something may be in the proper amount...its effects can cause our systems to become flooded.

Too much sugar floods the pancreas and makes it run poorly. Too much of just about any food can flood our body's cells and overload them with fat. Too much alcohol, tobacco or any drug floods the brain and inhibits proper body and mind function.

An excess of sexual stimulation, whether visual or sensual, can flood the centers that control the body's chemistry and impair the ability to reason. Any who observe adolescents, and survived their own adolescence, can testify to that.

Almost any day you can observe TV's Dr. Phil chiding a wayward husband, wife or otherwise committed individual with the words, "What were you thinking?"

If they are truthful, and understand human nature, they will reply, "I wasn't thinking...my brain was flooded...my self-control choke wasn't working."

The chorus of one of my favorite gospel songs reads, "He touched me, Oh! He touched me. And Oh! the joy that floods my soul. Something happened, and now I know, He touched me and made me whole."

When the Lord is in charge of one's life, you can be sure that the Automatic Choke is engaged, and adjusted for maximum efficiency. The only flooding will be the overwhelming flow of joy and blessings which He has promised.

Is your life running smoothly? Is your Automatic Choke engaged? Then drive on.

PARABLE OF THE
SILENT SHEPHERD

I've been thinking a lot about leadership and followship since I became the best friend of Suzy Q Mahoney. Suzy is the Black Labrador Retriever (mostly) that I adopted...or did she adopt me? Some days it's hard to tell.

I've written about the procession of other creatures that have had me as their pet over the years, and the lessons I have taught...and learned...while trying to maintain the proper relationship with them. Suzy Q is the current beneficiary of this accumulation of wisdom... with occasional tips gained from The Dog Whisperer.

If you're not familiar with The Dog Whisperer, don't feel alone. I recognized the name to be one of those floating in the TV ether somewhere but had never seen the program, hosted by Cesar Millan on the National Geographic Channel, or read any of Millan's best-selling books.

According to Millan the most important factor in the task of training a dog to be a fully cooperating member of its new family is establishing who is in charge...whose will must be followed...whose commands must be obeyed...who is to be the pack leader.

Dogs, he points out are pack animals...not in the sense of being beasts of burden, but rather in that of being members of a more or less organized group, or pack. Their natural sense of security comes from understanding where they stand in the hierarchy...or "high-arky" as one dear friend used to say...of the group. That knowledge, when clearly established, gives them a confidence and feeling of purpose as they go through their day.

That knowledge went a long way toward explaining why our first dog-friend, Cody, took it upon himself to drag whoever happened to be holding his lead relentlessly through the neighborhood each time one attempted to take him for his daily "walks." In his insecurity, he instinctively knew that someone had to take charge of those expeditions, and, in that leadership vacuum, he would stage a coup d'état and take control.

In fairness to myself, however, let me point out that I only did what I had always seen other dog-walkers do, let the dog set the pace, usually at the extreme end of the lead, making its way wherever its nose, its digestive system and the radius of the lead dictated. Verrrrrrrry bad, says the Dog Whisperer. The person needs to take the role of Alpha Dog in the pack, set the pace, control the direction, even determine when it is acceptable to stop to transact puppy "business."

I'm beginning to learn how to convince Suzy that I am the one in charge...that she can count on me to make the decisions about when, where and how fast to go. She seems to be a lot more at ease and comfortable when she is convinced that I will take responsibility for those decisions.

That revelation about the nature of leadership has given me a whole new perspective on life. In the last few months, it has even affected my view of spiritual things.

In fact, while I was practicing a piece of music with the choir recently, it stirred up memories of some preparation I did years ago for a Sunday School lesson. The anthem was a new setting of the hymn verse "Savior, like a Shepherd Lead Us," and the study it called to mind was on Psalm Twenty-Three, the Psalm of the Good Shepherd.

In his description of the Good Shepherd, the Psalmist uses words that are strong and positive, indicating decisiveness and confidence...

He makes, leads, restores, guides, comforts, prepares, anoints. The only response required of the sheep is to follow, to lie down, to have no fear, to dwell.

Just as the Dog Whisperer seems to know and understand the nature and needs of dogs, the Silent Shepherd...or perhaps we could call Him the Sheep Whisperer...knows the nature and needs of us, His sheep. It's His job to lead and provide...it's our job to follow, to obey and be at peace.

❀

PARABLE OF FOOTPRINTS IN THE STRAND

I have already written about the fact that in the Worrill family lexicon the definitions of "vacation" and "beach" are the same: Pawleys Island. Pawleys Island, South Carolina is a small sliver of an island, about halfway up on the Atlantic side of what is called the Waccamaw Neck. The promoters of tourism call that area the Golden Strand.

In my idle curiosity about where the Golden Strand name came from, I did what I usually do. I checked out "strand" in my ancient American Heritage dictionary. As I guessed, and should have known, the strand is that part of a shoreline that marks the area of a beach between the high and low tide marks. And for me, the Pawleys Island strand is as good as golden.

After a number of Pawleys-less years, I returned there recently with my daughter Abby and her sweet family. And, as if there had been no time gap, I resumed my former practice of arising while the first fingers of dawn were just beginning to grasp the eastern horizon, as the sun prepared to climb over and start a new day.

I noticed that things have changed since those early days on the beach when I was younger, and early morning walks and jogs were something only for a few insomniacs, health nuts and a small number of those of us categorized as "morning people." Even at 5:30 and 6:00 there were already a dozen or so sets of footprints tracing their way across the strand, where I once could boast that mine were the only ones in sight.

Even at that, though, I was able to find plenty of pristine, cleanly-swept sand where the print of my steps was isolated from all others, giving me the sense that the Lord and I were there together... and alone. I have always found that a comforting time, full of personal significance.

On each walk I would eventually reach a time when I had to turn around and go back the way I came. Even with the distinctive footprints of joggers, power-walkers and "mosey-ers" now visible on the strand, I found that I could pick my footprints from among these evidences of other human sprinters, striders and strollers.

I was able to identify where my striding steps changed and the prints of both feet were together in places where I stopped to look at something, like a particular shell, or a piece of the tide's flotsam, or turned to take a photo...even one place where I stopped for a polite interchange with a crab, which was also out for its morning constitutional. I was able to reconstruct almost the entire morning's journey just by reading those footprints. I felt like a native guide following a trail through the wilderness.

In the silence of those morning excursions, accompanied only by the sounds of the surf and the occasional cry of a sea-bird, I recalled a comment my best friend from high school once shared with me. He offered the thought that the bond with a friend was a special relationship where conversation is largely unnecessary.

That's true in a way, isn't it? True friends don't need to entertain... or amuse...or engage in idle chatter. Talk is often not needed, either as a barrier to keep someone at a polite distance, or as a drawbridge to allow them nearer in case of emergencies.

I especially sense my friendship with the Lord on those solitary strolls on the strand.

Once again, as we kept companionship on those early walks, I mentally marveled at the wonders of His creation. The beauty of the clouds on the distant horizon as the sun experimented with a vast variety of colors and shapes...the daily offerings of shells, and parts of shells...the tinted dunes, pulsing to the vibrations of the sun's first light of day...all visions of the Lord's infinite creativity. Those, after all, are the footprints the Lord leaves on the strand.

Yes, those silent mornings, elbow to elbow with the Creator, are special to me.

PARABLE OF THE GRATITUDE ATTITUDE

Ever since I started teaching Sunday School, I have had a practice of collecting notes and quotations that I thought might make good illustrations. Some of them have been direct inspirations of the Spirit. Some have been blatantly lifted from the sermons, messages and writings of others. Some have been a combination of that inspiration and petty plagiarism.

When I sit down to write I often look back through these collected thoughts to find the starting place for a new work. I am continually surprised by the way the Spirit calls my attention to a particular idea...almost as if looking over my shoulder and whispering, "How about that one?" I'm accustomed to that by now, so it wasn't unusual when I noticed several notes today. For example:

Overheard at church, "My granddaughter came crying to me and said, 'Gran, tell Bubba to share.' I asked her, 'Do you know what share means?' 'Yes,' she said, 'it means *give it here.*'" Now, how is that for a thought starter?

That cute family anecdote struck me as an accurate example of how we pray on some occasions. Don't we all pray at times as if God has to be informed about some imagined ill, or wrong that has been done...as if He needed to be coaxed to intervene on our behalf? Am I the only one who sometimes prays as if I were an attorney, pleading my case before an unbiased and indifferent judge, hoping to sway Him to my way of thinking?

Another note, on the subject of Prayer, helped me develop the thought a little further. It dealt with the attitude with which one should approach the activity of prayer.

Not too long ago I purchased and installed a new printer/scanner/copier. When I plugged it into the computer, the magic of electronics took over and they shook hands, introduced themselves and agreed what their relationship would be. The responsibility of the printer wasn't to ask the computer for data, but merely to await the instructions and commands of the CPU...then to obey by printing out what the computer required.

Sometimes, I'm afraid, my prayers are like those of the little girl, designed to move the Lord to convince someone to "Give it here." It's as if an overly anxious printer was attempting to suck information through the cable from an unresponsive CPU.

My notes are liberally salted with selections from the tales of Lake Wobegon, reported each week on The Prairie Home Companion. One of my favorites is the story of Bruno, the fishing dog. After one lucky incident while wading in the lake, Bruno spent his life trying to catch one of the fish that regularly frequent the shallow water.

One day, after breaking through the screen door and gaining access to a wedding reception, he spotted the largest smoked salmon anyone had ever seen, placed elegantly on the table...just waiting for him. He bounded onto the table, snatched up the entire fish and escaped back through the screen door with his prize. The problem was that after only a few bites Bruno discovered that he didn't even like smoked salmon. The one thing he had hoped and prayed for all his life...in his canine way...and he didn't care for it after all. Aren't some of our answered prayers like that?

Finally, there's the quotation from Dr. Peter Marshall, who said that on one occasion after Thanksgiving was past, he had asked his wife, Katherine, to ask the blessing at mealtime. He said, "You'll have to say grace this time, because the Lord knows I'm not grateful for turkey hash."

Although I may not be able to respond positively to all of God's provision—after all, He did provide mosquitoes, rattlesnakes, fleas and asparagus...none of them among my favorites—that doesn't make them any less of a blessing intended by Him for us. Our prayers should reflect an attitude of gratitude for what He has provided and a willingness to unselfishly obey His instructions.

PARABLE OF THE
OBVIOUS OBVERSE

Come on, now. Which of us hasn't at one time or another reached a decision—whether alone or as part of a group— by the flip of a coin? We say, "Call it. Heads or tails?"

I'll bet you've never heard anyone in that situation say, "Call it. Obverse or reverse?" That is, unless you're in the company of a group of numismatists (you know, coin collectors). In those circles, it's well-known that the front side of most modern coins contains a portrait, or an illustration of some feature representing the character or nature of the country or principality offering the coin as legal tender. Because that likeness is usually the portrayal of a monarch or other figure of historical importance, the front side...or obverse...is called "heads."

A curious aspect of this specialized terminology is that, according to these numismatic guidelines, the set of commemorative quarters that have been circulated in the US over recent years could be said to represent a special case. Normally, the obverse side has the portrait— these quarters all bear the likeness of George Washington. However, the second rule says that the obverse of a series of coins has content that varies, or is different from that of other coins in the series—in this case each state in the union has its own content on the side opposite the likeness of ol' George.

Rule three is the tie breaker. It dictates that the side bearing the name of the country is usually considered the obverse when there is a conflict between the first two rules.

By the way, the actual definition of the word "obverse" isn't much help in this matter, because it comes from the Latin word *obversus*, meaning "to turn toward". In other words, by definition the obverse is merely the side facing the observer.

I'll bet you didn't know any of that, did you? Unless you're a coin geek, of course. (And I certainly mean that in the kindest way.) Whatever.

As is the case with many of the weird rabbit trails winding their way through my mind, this one was suggested by a recent conversation. My son-in-law has been sorting through several sacks of coins collected by his father years ago. They represented many denominations...and many nations...and were received from customers in the retail store his dad ran for many years.

All coins used as a medium of exchange will fall into one of two categories. They are either struck from a kind and amount of precious metal, with its value guaranteed by the issuing authority; or that authority stands as a "powerful guarantor of the continuing acceptance of token coins." Thus, the old, silver quarters each contained twenty-five cents worth of silver; whereas the current "sandwich" quarters, with no silver content, are guaranteed by the government to be redeemable for twenty-five cents worth of silver...at least in theory. Don't try to cash them in, however.

There is another characteristic of all US coins that I think is noteworthy. On the obverse, or front...or heads, if you prefer...is the identification of the authority behind the coin: the government of the United States. On the reverse...or tails....is, to the founders of our nation, the authority behind that government: "In GOD We Trust," they affirmed.

Precious metal coins can be de-valued, by trimming their edges and, thus, stealing some of the metal. That led to the scoring of the edges so such acts could be detected. Guaranteed value, or token, coins can be counterfeited, though their small value hardly makes that practical.

It is equally true that the spirit behind these coins can be counterfeit. The intention to serve the best interests of those being governed...to guarantee and maintain the value they rely upon...can be perverted. Likewise, many today counterfeit a genuine trust in the authority behind that government, the God of creation. In practice, they place their trust in the traditional obverse.

My question for you is this: Which side of the coin of Trust is *your* obverse? The side ruled by man's law...or God's? For the true Believer the obverse is obvious. At least, it should be. So...call it... "Heads or Tails?"

PARABLE OF THE PAINFUL PROBLEM

My wife Lyn was always the plant person of the family. When she graduated into the Kingdom, the Lord provided me with my Joyce, another plant person. I've said...and proved on more than one occasion...that I could kill a cactus. That's why my responsibility has always been as the hole-digger and pot-fetcher...not as the greens-keeper.

I was reminded of that character flaw the other day when I moved a collection of potted flora that had been in my way during some rearranging in the kitchen. In fact, this happened to be a varied group of cacti Lyn had nursed over a period of ten years or so. I had neglected them for over a year, and now those that still showed signs of life were giving their final gasp.

As I performed last rites on one cactus before consigning it to plant heaven, it revived long enough to punish my misbehavior by leaving several tiny and nearly invisible spines in my fingers. I told myself, "It serves you right for being so neglectful," and continued with my task. That wasn't the end of the cactus' revenge, however. For quite a while that day every time I touched something those invisible little darts gave me a twinge of pain...until I stopped what I was doing, searched out each one and removed it.

Isn't it amazing how something so seemingly insignificant and petty can take control of one's mind...interrupt the whole body's activity...distract one from performing meaningful duties...until something is done to eliminate or control the pain? And the urgency seems to increase at bedtime, when the diversions and distractions of the day are gone and those aches and pains have our full attention. I can't count the times when my sleep has suffered because of a splinter, a toothache or a sore toe. When one body part hurts, the whole body is miserable.

So... what's the deal with pain? People who are not well acquainted with Him often ask, "How can a God who claims to be so loving allow us to suffer pain and death?" What's the purpose of pain, anyway?

In the first place, it's important to understand that humans are specifically designed to register pain. Pain is the body's alarm system to alert us to the fact that something is wrong. Just as a home's alarm system warns of intruders trying to gain entrance, the body has its nervous system to sound the alert that we are under attack by some outside threat.

I once had an acquaintance who had diabetes, which affected the nerves in his extremities. One foot had to be amputated, because he didn't feel any pain when he damaged several of his toes. Pain isn't always a tool of the enemy.

In a recent discussion of grief, the question was raised about how there could be any possible benefit from the pain felt by the grieving one. "People keep telling me to get over it, that the pain will pass and I'll be my old self in time. I'll *never* be my old self again. I'm not sure I want to."

Physical pain is the body's way of alerting us that something is wrong and needs to be taken care of. Mental and emotional pain were given to us to help us deal with other types of issues with which we need to deal.

With physical pain we will usually resort to our favorite home remedy...and eventually, if that proves ineffective and the pain persists, we will often consult a specialist. Why are we not as attentive when we are afflicted with emotional pain, like that experienced with the loss of one we love? It is useless...even harmful...for us to sit there and bear the pain, hoping it'll go away in time.

When the Lord allows us to feel emotional pain, it is with the desire that we will reach the point of coming to Him, the specialist in dealing with our deepest and most painful problems. That pain isn't intended to torture us for bad choices or misplaced affections, but simply to alert us to the fact that we need Him...and, when we call upon Him, He is ready and able to bear that pain away.

PARABLE OF THE PROVIDENTIAL COINCIDENCE

"One day as I sat brooding, sad and melancholy, a voice came to me out of the gloom saying, 'Cheer up. Things could be worse.' So, I cheered up. And, sure enough, *things got worse!*"

When I was a young man in the printing and advertising business, I remember receiving a card with this quotation printed on it. It was a little cynical, of course, but I thought it was funny. I passed out a lot of those cards. Everyone got a laugh from them.

A philosopher might point out that there is a logical flaw in the quotation that is sometimes referred to by those acquainted with the art of argument, as the *post hoc* fallacy...more properly, *post hoc, ergo propter hoc*...after this, therefore because of this. In other words, just because a thing occurs *after* an event it doesn't necessarily follow that it was *caused* by that event. In this case, he would say, it wasn't the act of cheering up that made things worse. That was merely a coincidence.

My Mom wasn't a philosopher or a psychologist, but she was a mom, and that's almost the same thing. Whenever one of us was sad, or having a bad day, she would advise us to find a distraction... something fun to do or think about...get our minds off whatever was disturbing us. And, coincidence or not, that usually did the trick.

We all have times, however brief, when we are touched by periods of sadness and melancholy...and when those occasions occur the prospect of things getting worse is not nearly as humorous, as that little card implies. I know from personal experience, because I've had some of those feelings myself from time to time.

Whenever I've had an episode of that hollow sadness, the Lord has helped me find plenty to keep me laughing, and I've found that to be a very effective treatment on those occasions. As I've written before, there's nothing better than a good laugh to keep the adversary and his imps at bay.

I had this proved yet again recently when I was having "one of those days." I really needed a distraction. So, I said "To heck with it," and went to see a movie. Not a puny, TV screen-size movie, but an honest-to-goodness, big-screen, theater-sound movie.

The one I selected was the re-make of the old John Wayne movie, "True Grit." It had all the necessary elements for a perfect diversion... compelling story...Academy Award caliber actors, directors, story, and so on. All the action, noise and beautiful scenery were beginning to have the desired effect, when I suddenly recognized the background music. "Hold to God's Unchanging Hand," "Leaning on the Everlasting Arms," "What a Friend We Have in Jesus." Not only three of my favorite hymns, but three statements that spoke to me as if they had been selected specifically for me on this particular occasion. I had to laugh...and shed a few tears at the same time.

I know...there are many who will say this has to be purely coincidental. A movie like this takes months and even years to produce. There are stories to be written and revised, screenplays to be developed, actors hired, sets built, film shot and edited; the entire production pulled together, promoted and distributed to theaters, showings scheduled.

One doesn't have to be familiar with many of my writings to recognize that I'm not one who puts much stock in the idea of coincidence. But some may say, it *has* to be a coincidence that I made a last-minute decision to see this particular movie on the day and at the specific time that I needed to hear those reassuring messages in song. Doesn't it?

I don't believe that for a minute. This isn't the first time the Lord has reminded me that I'm not alone. He has made His fellowship very real to me...demonstrated His loving care and concern in ways that are so evident that it makes me smile, and sometimes weep, to realize His providence.

God knows exactly what troubles and difficulties you're facing. And He has a providential coincidence ready to prove He cares for you. Just look around...you'll see it.

PARABLE OF THE HEAVENLY MATCH

It's difficult to find inspiration and encouragement in the daily news reports these days. It seems that unless an item contains details of destruction, murder and/or mayhem it has little chance to be selected for review by the news-hungry public

And yet every once in a great while there is a news nugget that revives the hope that maybe things are not so bad after all. Something that provides a wonderful example of how things could and should be if we would only take it to heart.

There was just such a story recently from the Woodland West Animal Hospital in Tulsa, Oklahoma. It was the tale of Tanner and Blair and their unusual relationship.

Tanner is a two-year-old Golden Retriever who was born blind. Apparently, the stress of trying to cope with his condition was causing daily seizures. During those seizures Tanner would lose control of bodily functions and would wallow in the mess that caused. His second owner couldn't deal with those problems and brought Tanner to Woodland. At first the staff was convinced that the only kind thing to do was to put him to sleep. The seizures became more frequent.

Blair is a street mutt of indefinite origin, shy and skittish, and unsociable after being shot. Her prospects for finding a home were slim because of her withdrawn behavior. At least that was the case until she was placed in the yard at the same time as Tanner.

These two misfits immediately became inseparable friends. As time went by, the result of their friendship was that Tanner became less stressed...his seizures decreased and finally ceased altogether. Blair lost her shyness and became more friendly. She even took on the role of care-giver to her blind companion, becoming a dog's guide dog... leading Tanner around the yard on a leash.

They have been transformed from a pair of misfits with no prospects for normal lives, to an inspiring example of what life should be like for us all. Theirs is a suggestion that there may be such a thing as a match made in heaven...even for dogs. After all, how likely is it that these two would just happen to be there, same place, same time, with just the right combination of needs and skills to make the ideal relationship?

Of course, there are those who'll prefer to call this just a lucky coincidence, but not me. I have too strong a sense of the Presence of God in my life to believe in coincidence.

I've written before about my belief that we are each born with a complete set of "software" to equip us for every event that we will encounter in our lives. As we approach each set of circumstances, we have a choice of how we'll deal with them...and whether or not we will discover and apply the proper program for a successful experience.

I don't have any problem whatsoever believing that the story of Tanner and Blair can serve as an illustration of how we each should approach each day of our life. Whether one is a Tanner or a Blair, there is a counterpart who needs the skills and abilities one can offer...and who has the skills and abilities to meet even the smallest need.

There is another important lesson for Believers in this story. Neither Tanner not Blair was out looking for solutions for their problems. They were suffering through them...desiring relief, but had not the knowledge or ability to seek help. That help came completely aside from their efforts.

It was up to Tanner and Blair to recognize and take advantage of their opportunity. Once they acted, their bond of friendship was the natural outcome.

Whenever I'm tempted to become stressed about my situation... when circumstances make me want to withdraw and give up...the Spirit always reminds me that God has a plan, and a process, designed for me...a heavenly match...and He will bring me through. He has one for you, too.

PARABLE OF THE LEVEL, THE SQUARE AND THE PLUMB LINE

I suppose it comes to us all at some time or another, but I'll always remember one of my earliest realizations that there is a big difference between the real world and the ideal world of which we all so fondly dream. It wasn't during one of those earth-shaking, "Ahah!" moments, either.

It came in the midst of performing one of those mundane chores we find on our "To Do" lists at one time or another. In this case it occurred as we were preparing to put up new wallpaper in the kitchen of our home in Atlanta.

The Handyman's Guide instructed us that after the wall has been prepped and our wallpaper is ready, we should take a plumb line and "snap" a reference line on the wall at the beginning point. In other words, apply chalk to the string, pull it out from the wall and release it so it leaves a chalk line on the wall from ceiling to floor. Easy enough.

Here's where my lesson in reality came in. It was at that time that it became clear to me that it's unrealistic to expect any two adjacent surfaces in the typical home to be either level, square or plumb. How's that for a real-life lesson?

Throughout life we find ourselves constantly having to make adjustments and accommodations to our plans because of those little failures...those slight, or not so slight imperfections...of others. "What's the big deal about that?" you might ask. "Everyone knows that nobody's perfect. Get over it."

And that is exactly my point. If nobody's perfect, what's the purpose for having rules, laws and standards that are impossible to live up to? What's wrong with simply letting every person "do what is right in his own eyes"?

By way of introduction to a course in Business Law, the professor, "Judge" Aldrich, told the class, "In order to maintain a well-ordered society it is essential to remember that a man's freedom to swing his fist leaves off where his neighbor's nose begins." And that, in a nutshell, is the intended function of all laws, rules and standards...to define a standard of expected behavior and maintain a separation between fists and noses...to protect each of us from the misbehavior of others.

A prominent figure in the news was heard to say that he believed in living by the Golden Rule. I once heard a radio evangelist say "The Golden Rule is to Christian living as 'Twinkle, twinkle, little star' is to Astronomy." The Golden Rule is a good beginning, but it's woefully inadequate as a philosophy of life.

A friend told me the other day that he and his wife tried to live according to the Ten Commandments...and isn't this what God expects of us all? The only trouble with that as a goal, as the Bible points out, is the Commandments constitute a standard impossible for mankind in our selfish, unregenerated state to live up to.

What's the point of having a law that is impossible to keep? Why build a fence that won't keep offenders from crossing a line? Who'll obey an unreasonably low speed limit on a super highway? How are these restrictions supposed to protect us, or make us better?

Again, the Bible has the answer. The Ten Commandments clearly indicate what it will take for us to meet God's requirements for His blessings and for fellowship with Him. He is perfect...man is not. Therefore, the Law is designed to show us there is no way we can hope to be good enough…obedient enough…worthy enough of His blessings and His fellowship…without His help.

The sad fact is that, until we begin to realize how far short, we fall from measuring up to His standards, we will…by our human nature… always view our efforts as pretty close…nearly good enough to warrant His blessing. And, isn't "close enough" good enough?

Just as a conscientious builder cannot be pleased with a structure that is not level, square and in plumb…and will tear out and rebuild any elements that fall short of those standards…God applies His measures to each of us and must, by His nature, destroy anything that falls short of His perfection. As much as He loves His creation, He will not accept any flaw or blemish.

If it were possible for us to make our lives level, square and in plumb through simple obedience to the Ten Commandments, Jesus would never have had to come in order to save us from God's judgment. God's Law defines the offences of which we are guilty. The perfect sacrifice of Jesus was offered to pay the fine for our failures under that law.

When we accept His terms, His Spirit instructs and guides in rebuilding those parts of our lives that violate His code and leads us into faithful compliance. Never again need we be fearful or suspicious of the level, the square and the plumb line.

PARABLE OF THE EXPIRATION DATE

I'm not sure, but I think I'm in trouble. That's why I wanted to give you this bit of warning. If you should come to visit me and discover my cold, lifeless corpse curled into a fetal position and lying on the kitchen floor, it may be because I violated one of the basic safety rules of modern consumers: I didn't pay proper attention to the expiration dates on my food products.

Let me give you a little background.

My sweet life companion of fifty years was a great shopper...a master of the couponers' craft and dedicated practitioner of sales shopping. She kept our freezer and pantry shelves stocked with treasures purchased at bargain prices, with some items stacked three or four deep. So deep, in fact, that some of them disappeared from the homemaker's radar for months...even years...at a time.

Canned goods and dry goods have always been considered fair game for long-term storage in our household, and...as long as the top wasn't swollen and the seams weren't leaking...the contents were considered safe to cook and consume. Dedicated survivalists could exist for months from that stock of goods without ever having to leave the house.

Of course, there were certain perishables which couldn't be wedged into the packed-solid freezer. They were either consumed in good time or tossed out when they became spoiled. (I've always enjoyed the line from the play "The Odd Couple" when one character described the food in his refrigerator. "If it's brown, it's cheese...if it's green it's roast beef.") Over fifty years we disposed of a lot of brown, green and flocked food that was purchased at bargain prices.

When I began life for the first time as a single, my loving daughters came over to the house and made a noble effort to weed out this bountiful store of foodstuffs to bring it down to a more manageable size. And, to their credit, they made many trips to the curb with items that were obviously no longer useable...at least, according to their expiration dates.

That was more than two years ago. There are still cans and containers of soups and sauces, vegetables and condiments that haven't yet worked their way to the front of the line to be prepared and consumed. And don't even ask about the freezer.

I do my best to keep these vast stores of goods turning over. Really, I do. But there's only so much that will be used up in preparing meals for one. And let me be honest here...I really hate the idea of throwing out something that may still be perfectly good.

"Give it to some needy family," you say? Yeah...and run the risk of being sued for causing a lethal case of food poisoning? Not likely. "But there are children in Somalia that are starving..." They're probably the same ones that were starving when I was a child and wouldn't eat my green beans and squash. And they'd probably sue me, too.

Seriously, though, I know this is a problem. I was reminded of that today as I read an article about, of all things, expiration dates. It was very troubling for a saver like me. I'll bet that even you would experience a grumble or two in the digestive system if you knew what I now know.

The good news is that those expiration dates on the can are guidelines and aren't like little time bombs that go off on a pre-determined date and render the contents deadly. The old rules for judging safety still apply. If a can leaks or looks as if it's about to blow, it probably is. Throw it out.

When you open the can and what's supposed to be liquid isn't... throw it out. If it smells funny or has a peculiar color or looks as if an alien life form has taken over, throw it out. And the same goes for dry goods...if in doubt, well...you know.

This whole train of thought started me thinking about something else, though. What if each of the people you see as you walk down the street, or those you sit next to in church, came with an expiration date stamped on their foreheads. The mother of well-known Southern author Celestine Sibley said of some people who seemed peculiar, "They're not bad, they're just turned funny." Would we treat folks differently...alter our expectations for them...if we knew when they were expected to "go bad"...to turn funny?

There is the old expression about someone being "past his/her prime." Is that like saying they're past their "best if used by" date? Are we inclined to discount others because we suspect their expiration date has passed?

The whole purpose of proper handling, preparation and storage techniques is to extend an item's useful life. Have you ever considered that applies to people, too? God has.

The Lord has already put into operation a Plan to salvage, preserve and extend the useful life of each one who comes to Him in faith and dependence upon His Grace. Not only does He do away with our old expiration date...the date when we go bad and should be thrown out...but He offers an eternal guarantee of our usefulness according to His Will.

So...tell me, do you know your expiration date, or has it been extended eternally?

PARABLE OF THE THINGS WE VALUE

I read two articles this morning about several interesting discoveries made recently. The first was about a man who has discovered on his property a nearly complete skeleton of a 14,000-year-old Mastodon. There were pictures of him holding a five-foot-long femur from the long-extinct beast. Since it was uncovered on his own land, he apparently has legal right to it, so he is collecting all the bones in his home. He says he'll probably need to build on another room in which to keep the entire specimen once it has been reassembled. He still hopes to find the gigantic animal's skull.

The second article dealt with a tremendous bit of debris that washed up on the Oregon coast a day or so ago. A floating dry-dock measuring 66 feet long, 19 feet wide and 7 feet high was finally washed onto the beach after being sighted in the surf several days earlier. It had a sign and markings in Japanese, indicating that it was probably some of the debris swept out to sea by the tsunami in Japan last year. Authorities are still trying to identify its origin. This is just one example of the arrival of the flotsam and jetsam set afloat by the massive natural disaster.

There has been, and will continue to be for some time, a regular appearance of this debris which represents items once owned and valued by residents of the Japanese cities struck by the irresistible tide. Some other things reported in the article include mountains of clothing, a soccer ball and a Harley-Davidson motorcycle.

As I thought about each of these finds, I tried to imagine the value they represented to their original owners. Those immense bones represented life itself to that mastodon all those Millenia ago. If that creature could be interviewed about what those bones meant to him and what he thought about the person currently in their possession, I can imagine him saying, "Those bones were, like, a part of me, y'know, and I hope he'll, like, take good care of them. I'm just sayin', y'know?"

To that mastodon the bones were invaluable...to their new owner they are a curiosity, possibly worth a lot of money, but certainly not something he couldn't live without. They would be valued even differently by scientists who might study them with hopes of making new discoveries about pre-historic life and death...and how these discoveries help us understand ourselves and our place in the scope of time.

The unbelievable flood of debris that daily arrives on our shores from Japan is a different matter altogether. The vast majority represents items that were part of the everyday life and livelihood of an entire population of people. Their loss may not have been a matter of life and death for their unfortunate owners, but it did strike a devastating blow to their lifestyle...likely altering their lives beyond the possibility of recovery.

The discovery of those bones didn't affect the life or the life choices of the long-gone mastodon. But they are an indication of a life successfully lived. They also serve to remind us that nothing is permanent...the most successful life will someday come to an end.

The accumulated belongings gradually finding their way 4,000 miles across the ocean also have a lesson for us. They teach about how to judge the things that are important in life. What can be swept away so easily in moments should be held lightly, with open fingers...not clutched with a death-grip as if it is essential for a joyful life.

What's more, those bones and the tsunami's deposits also remind us that many of life's greatest treasures come to us unbidden, suddenly discovered before us or under our very feet. These things occur around us all the time...but they often go undetected because we don't take the time to pay attention to our surroundings as we rush from one urgent project to the next.

What are some of the things that you value? Has your curiosity lead you to some treasure you didn't know was there? Have you spent your time accumulating things that can be taken from you by the floods of circumstance...or have you been the recipient of valued things taken from others?

I recommend investing your life in people...accumulating memories...developing ideas to share with others...helping them along their way. Then, even when life comes to an end, something of substance will be left behind to be enjoyed and experienced by others. Don't value too highly those things which can be removed by the tide...every important item can be replaced.

When you learn to look at things through God's eyes, you'll find it much easier to place the proper value on things...and people... around you. "Seek first the kingdom of God and His righteousness, and all these things shall be added to you." (Matthew 6:33, NKJV)

PARABLE OF THE POWER SOURCE

I was unpacking from a recent trip to the beach...*the* beach in our family is Pawleys Island, South Carolina, of course. As I was re-distributing the contents of the various suitcases, bags, boxes and totes, I realized how utterly dependent we are upon one modern necessity. From a number of compartments, pouches, nooks and crannies I assembled nearly a dozen different types and sizes of cords, wires and cables.

I had cords for two cameras, for transferring photos from the camera to my computer. There were two cords to perform the same vital connection for two eBook readers...and one of those had an additional piece that allows one to re-charge the device's internal battery from a conventional wall plug.

There were two cords for re-charging my electric razor and my cell phone. I surely wouldn't want to forget either of those necessities for modern civilized life.

And finally, there were the two cords needed to power and re-charge my laptop computer. In all fairness, I didn't go to the beach to play computer games or maintain my Facebook page...nor to conduct any type of non-vacation activities. I took my laptop so I could continue my habit of writing these parables several times a week. Really.

Last but not least in this gadget tally were two types of battery chargers. There is one for each of the two types of rechargeable batteries my various devices...including my battery-operated toothbrush...require.

A good friend of mine once predicted, "We're headed for the day when whoever controls the manufacture and distribution of batteries can rule the world." Add battery chargers and power cords and I think we're there.

I was working with my son-in-law the other day, helping build a new playset for his grandson. There were over 200 individual pieces to be assembled, using screws, nuts and bolts and endless bags of lock washers. About halfway through the afternoon he said, "When this cordless screwdriver runs down, we'll be out of luck, because I can't find the re-charger." Having to hand drive all those screws and bolts would have added days...and liberal applications of liniment...to the amount of time required to complete the task.

All these marvelous labor-saving devices have made life easier and more enjoyable in many ways, that's true. We can accomplish today things we perhaps would never have considered in the manual-powered days of yore. However, we do seem to be at the mercy of those indispensable umbilicals connecting us to sources of power, don't we? Even in the wi-fi world in which we now live, at some point in the chain of devices, something has to be plugged in to a power source... or attached to a battery pack.

I find it interesting that we can be so attentive to the needs of our iPods, iPads and Smart Phones...our eBooks, MP3's, PDQ's and I don't know what all...and pay so little attention to the most essential of all sources of power. The power that keeps our gadgets working properly is nothing compared to the Power that our spirits require for the proper operation of a life.

Mankind has attempted to provide for itself the power to sustain a satisfying and productive life, without success. The results are always disappointing and never last long.

The Lord offers us the only complete and effective source of Power through His Holy Spirit. There is a catch, however. A successful connection to that Power requires an adaptor...and that perfect adaptor is Jesus. Accepting Him as your only acceptable power source gives a whole new meaning to the expression "Put Jesus in *charge* of your life," don't you think?

PARABLE OF THE EXTRA SENSE

I once heard a physicist suggest a theory that reminded me of that corny old line from the early sci-fi movies, where the lead character looks thoughtfully at his/her companions and says, "I know it seems crazy…but it just might work." The theory was related to the transmission of electrical impulses over long distances.

As I recall it, the theory was that electrical waves, once generated, go out in all directions from the point of origin and continue forever. The idea was that if only it were possible to produce a receiver with enough power to amplify even the tiniest ripple of electrical energy it would be a simple matter to listen to even the earliest wireless messages ever transmitted.

According to that theory, even the earliest successful efforts of Guglielmo Marconi at transmitting wireless messages over long distances could be pulled from the ether, amplified and re-broadcast. There was a time…even during my lifetime…when that seemed an outrageous and unrealistic idea.

Since then, however, scientists have transmitted and received messages over millions of miles through space, communicating with unmanned satellites at the outer limits of our solar system. So, what's so strange about accidentally picking up impulses that have been bouncing around for a hundred years or so?

A few days ago, I was on the road following the persistent urging of the faithful electronic traveling companion I've nicknamed Ado Annie...after the young lady in "Oklahoma" who "can't say no." I thought about the fact that I was receiving and responding to a steady stream of impulses being beamed from a satellite hundreds of miles away. Not only that, but those impulses had to elbow their way through crowds of similar impulses coursing on their way to countless other receivers...in countless other locations...with countless other communications.

Now...consider this. We know national and international intelligence agencies are able to receive and sort out communications from all over the world, and through complicated computer programs identify and isolate specific types of messages. If that is possible with fresh, currently transmitted signals, why couldn't it be possible to increase the amplification and improve the tuning to trap impulses from other time periods?

Let's take this fancy just a little further. If it is true, as many scientists believe, that all brain activity is through electro-chemical impulses...and if those impulses possess the same properties that mechanically produced electrical impulses have...perhaps our thoughts and imaginations are being broadcast into the ether, to join all the other energy waves pulsing through the universe.

Scientists and inventors have devised equipment and systems to collect radio transmissions. Shouldn't it be possible to create a receiver to pick up and interpret at least some of these brain transmissions? I have no idea, and it seems awfully far-fetched...but *it just might work,* right?

I'm not aware of any research on the subject, but could it be that there are some individuals with especially sensitive receivers in their brains which can accept and respond to these brain waves escaping the skulls of those around them? What if this was the explanation for those who claim to have Extra-Sensory Perception? If Marconi could do it...and Ado Annie can do it...why not some person with a properly focused mental capacity? Intriguing thought, isn't it?

Do you have a headache yet from all that theorizing? Well, like that other character in "Oklahoma" I think I've "gone about as far as I can go" with this line of thinking.

Let me tell you what I do know from personal experience. I'm not concerned about ever being able to receive and process either ancient or modern electrical impulses...as interesting as the concept may be. I have made it a practice to try keeping my mental receiver tuned to receive transmissions of a spiritual nature...transmissions direct from the Creator of the universe.

Without benefit of antennas and banks of sophisticated equipment, the Lord has given me the ability to receive His words of instruction, comfort and cheer. His prophet Isaiah tells me, "Thine ears shall hear a word behind thee saying, this is the way, walk ye in it, when ye turn to the right hand, and when ye turn to the left." (Isaiah 30:21)

No, I don't require a Smart Phone with a peppy ringtone...no noise-cancelling Blue Tooth device handing on my ear...no hands-free speaker phone with wi-fi capabilities. I came already equipped with an extra sense which enables me to receive His messages at any time of night or day...anywhere in the universe I may happen to be. The activation fee was paid for by Jesus and I have a lifetime subscription, with free up-dates.

Are you part of the Extra Sense network? If not, I can show you how easy it is to get signed up today.

PARABLE OF THE LOST CAPTAIN

I've always loved words and admired the proper use of them. I give most of the credit for that fascination to my parents, neither of whom had any special credentials in the area of English usage. My mother did earn a high school diploma, but my dad...an eighth-grade drop-out...gained most of his knowledge of spelling, grammar and punctuation while working in a print shop, setting type, proofreading and later writing advertising copy.

I grew up hearing proper English spoken around the house, and, although I was always a little fuzzy about the proper handles for the rules of grammar and parts of speech, I could almost always identify what was correct simply because it "sounded right." It also helped that I worked for my dad from time to time, also setting and proofreading type in his direct mail printing shop.

Mom's family moved to Southeast Alabama from Atlanta about the time she entered high school, when it's difficult to be the "new kid." In her English class she had to learn several poems and give recitations before the class, and apparently did them well enough that one of them was the source of the nickname she carried all through high school. I think it was from a poem called Billy Brag, but I may be mistaken. After that all her school friends...even her family...called her Bill.

Another poem she apparently learned and recited was *The Ballad of the Tempest*, by James T. Fields. The only reason I happen to remember that one is that, whenever she became what we used to call "bumfuzzled," ...you know, disoriented or confused...or when things just weren't going the way they should, she would loudly proclaim, "'We are lost!' the captain shouted..."

Recently, that line came to me and after all these decades I decided to look it up. (Isn't Google marvelous?) It's a Victorian poem about a family aboard ship during a storm. About half-way through, sure enough, there was the line I remembered:

As thus we sat in darkness
Each one busy with his prayers,
"We are lost!" the captain shouted,
As he staggered down the stairs.

This daisy-chain of thoughts began one Sunday while the pastor was speaking on the passage in Luke 19, where Jesus spots Zacchaeus the tax collector, sitting up in that sycamore tree. After spending the day with him, Jesus informs the crowd that salvation has come to his house, because "The Son of Man has come to seek and save that which was lost." There's that word "lost," again.

The word translated "lost" is the Greek perfect participle *apollumi*, and refers to an action completed in the past but with ongoing results. It means to destroy fully; die, lose, mar, perish. The Bible assures us that this is the natural condition of all mankind in our sinful state. We are lost, fully destroyed, marred and doomed to perish.

Mom's poem doesn't leave the unfortunate seafarers in despair, however. Everything works out well in the end. In the next stanza it goes on in true Victorian fashion:

But his little daughter whispered,
As she took his icy hand,
"Isn't God upon the ocean,
Just the same as on the land?"

Just as the characters in Mom's recitation saw their confidence in God's protection and providence justified, Jesus gives us clear and convincing testimony of the persistent nature of His desire for all to be restored to Him. The words translated "seek" and "save" are in a tense that indicates they are not restricted by time limits. It is God's nature to seek at all times, without condition...to save at all times, without limitation.

His seeking isn't a once and for all proposition. It has no time limit or expiration. God doggedly pursues each disobedient individual, intending of bring him to a realization of his sinful state. It's His desire to save...the Greek word *Soso* means to deliver, protect, heal, preserve, make whole.

So, here's the picture: The Bible describes us as being fully destroyed, marred and doomed to perish because of our selfish disobedience. Jesus describes Himself as engaged in a timeless search for us...with a limitless desire to bring us back, heal and make us whole again so that we may be preserved for Him.

Whether we remain Lost and doomed to perish like that Captain...or allow ourselves to be found, delivered and preserved according to the desire of Jesus...is a choice left to us. Though He seeks us relentlessly, He never forces us to accept His offer to restore us.

So...what'll you have? Lost and doomed...or sought and saved? I choose "Saved!"

PARABLE OF THE WELL-WORN WORD

The ability to read and write with understanding is among the great gifts of civilization. Perhaps the only greater gift is the ability to express our thoughts and feelings through spoken language. Without these precious gifts, each individual in each generation would face the task of "re-inventing the wheel" for himself. We'd probably still be living in caves...but wouldn't know what to call that hole in the ground.

I clearly recall sitting in the living-room in our white brick house on Willowood Circle in the Atlanta suburb of Kirkwood. I was tightly wedged into an armchair next to Mom as she patiently...for the most part...introduced me—with much weeping and gnashing of teeth, I must admit—to Dick and Jane, Sally and the baby, Spot and Fluff as they ran, jumped, sat, fell, cried and threw the ball. Oh! Oh! Oh! It was a long time before I could stand the thought of Dick and Jane and that yellow house of theirs with the white shutters and trim. But eventually we became friends.

In spite of that rocky beginning in the wonderful world of the written word, I eventually became a solid convert. I've written before about the fact that my favorite activity...second only to being outside playing with my friends...was sitting down with a Zane Grey western or one of my parents' Book of the Month Club offerings and spending a lazy afternoon reading.

I've learned that there are at least two kinds of readers...those who believe that books are like the "good" furniture, to be kept spotless and looking like new; and those who believe that a book is a thing to be handled and used up, with pages worn and marked, with favorite passages underlined and personal notes in the margins. I fit somewhere between those two extremes.

When I read a book...whether fiction or non, for enjoyment or as a casual pastime...I generally don't find a need to mark or write in it. I tend to read the way I walk through the neighborhood with Suzy Q, purposefully pacing along to get the job done...enjoying the sights and sounds along the way, but not leaving a trail behind.

When reading for information, however, whether for my own improvement or for the purpose of sharing that information with others, I am inclined to mark meaningful passages with underscores and arrows, and tiny notes...illegible, perhaps, to all but myself...in the margins and spaces between paragraphs.

I once had a professor who said, "I wouldn't give a nickel for a book that didn't have any writing or marks in it." In his view, if a book's contents didn't move one to mark thoughts for emphasis, to aid in recall or to express agreement or opposing opinions it couldn't be much good.

I thought about these things as I read an article in the Georgia Baptist newspaper, The Christian Index. There was a quotation from a pastor who, before preparing a eulogy for a funeral service in his church, had a practice of thumbing through the Bible of the deceased one. He said that often gave him a clear insight into the heart and mind of the one being remembered.

My brother-in-law, David Jones, himself a retired pastor who has officiated all the family's weddings and funerals for most of the past fifty years, introduced me to this practice when he prepared to preach at my dad's funeral nearly twenty years ago. He gleaned many meaningful thoughts and impressions from that well-worn Scofield Reference Bible that Dad had used during his last thirteen years of lay ministry. I inherited that Bible and have added almost twenty years' worth of my own notes, quotes and thoughts to what Dad had inscribed.

As a result of thirty-five years as a Sunday School teacher and a lifetime of church attendance and participation, I have accumulated quite a library of Bibles and Bible reference volumes. I've lost track of the number of translations of the New Testament and the whole Bible in my possession. And all of those that I've used as regular references have notes and markings in them. There are hardly two consecutive pages in my pocket testament without notations.

Please don't misunderstand me. I don't mean this as any sort of "Oh, what a good boy am I!" commentary. These notes and references aren't in any way an indication of my outstanding holiness and spiritual wisdom. To me, they are an ever-present reminder that the Bible is truly the Living Word...that the Holy Spirit continually inhabits that Word and imparts inspiration and wisdom to all those who will read that Word with open heart and willing mind.

My advice to Brother Dave, or whoever has to cobble together a eulogy for me, is to not be dismayed by the many notes and markings in my favorite copies and editions of the Word. The historian and writer Ken Burns would have trouble squeezing them into a thirty-hour documentary. Instead, just say, "Jack loved the Lord and His Word, and he made note of many conversations they had while he was reading that well-worn Word."

I was amused by the bumper sticker that read, "Have you read any Good Book lately?" How about you? Have you read your Bible lately? Does it look like new, or is it well-worn? If someone thumbed through your favorite copy of the Word, would they get an insight into your spiritual walk? If not, I promise you that today's not too late to start wearing it out.

PARABLE OF THE CRITICAL PATH

About a year ago I began to be involved in something that is quite new for me. The planning and preparation of meals was something for which I have had very little hands-on experience. Other than an occasional Saturday morning breakfast, or my assumed role as the Breakfast Chef during our family weeks at the beach, my previous kitchen knowledge was gained purely from my status as a casual, if not curious, observer.

In all fairness I must also point out that I came by that culinary indifference quite honestly. As I have written before, my dad's philosophy was that one should stick to those things he could do well and leave to others the things at which they excelled.

True to the example of many of his generation, Dad carried this to the limit when it came to "women's work." Cleaning, cooking and other household affairs, although subject to supervision...and occasional critique...were not things in which he took a great deal of interest. When left to his own devices, Dad's idea of cooking was to heat a can of Gebhardt's Chili in a pot of water and eat it out of the can. Simple. Easy. No fuss, muss or bother. End of story.

When it became clear that it was time for me to take more responsibility for meals, therefore, my prime role-model for being

Head of the House was absolutely no help whatsoever. I was on my own. Not to worry. I had watched it done hundreds of times. How hard could it be?

In my typical manner—call it Obsessive Compulsive, or even Anal Retentive, if you wish—I tackled the task. 1. Decide on the week's meals. Check. 2. Look up recipes, scour pantry for necessary mystic ingredients. Check. 3. Search for coupons, weekly specials. Check. 4. Stalk through grocery store(s) to find required items...at the best price. Check. 5. Bring home and group according to the day the items are to be prepared. Check.

Now, folks, in case you don't get it yet, I actually wrote out the above list and checked it off as each step was accomplished! How pitiful is that? When I admitted that to my daughters, they just nodded sympathetically and said encouraging things like, "That's all right, Dad, a lot of us had to do that in the beginning." Humbled, but encouraged nonetheless, I went doggedly on.

I mentioned the recipe for the major meal elements. Have you ever paid attention to how recipes are presented? First is the list of all the needed ingredients. Then most of them give the step-by-step instructions for carrying out the preparation. OK.

But here's what scorches my grits. When a meal involves several different recipes, how do you combine them so that everything comes out, ready to serve, at the same time? Housewives and chefs of every generation have learned how to do this, but what about me?

As a Georgia Tech graduate, I was acquainted with an Industrial Engineering technique called the Critical Path Method, a system for planning each element of a construction project so that it is on hand at exactly the time it is needed, theoretically allowing for the minimum delay. "That's it!" I thought. "I'll just use CPM to do my meal preparation. I'll make a Critical Path list."

"1. Take peas from freezer. 2. Boil water for macaroni. 3. While water boils, mix dry ingredients for Tilapia coating. 4. Turn oven to 450...." And on, and on. And, you know what? As silly as it looked when I came across that stupid list the other day, it really worked. (You don't look at all surprised. Of course, written-out list or not, that's what all experienced cooks do, isn't it?)

You know, I've spent all my life planning, organizing and arranging the details of my life to a fare-thee-well. In the end, I've come to the conclusion that the Lord designed me that way to provide me with an excess of "busy work" to keep me occupied while He set about working out His plan for me. I have no other explanation for the countless blessings I've received, in spite of myself.

Here's what I learned from all this: The Master Engineer's Critical Path always brings together the people and things that each Believer needs, at precisely the time they are needed. "Thy Word is a lamp unto my feet and a light unto my path." (Psalm 119:105)

We can not only avoid stumbling, but we can see where to step next. With each step on that path the next becomes visible. In times when we're impatient or our faith fails we may interfere with His schedule, but His plan is always perfect...His Critical Path precise. And when we get to the Table, everything's ready to enjoy.

PARABLE OF THE TWO-MINUTE DRILL

There was a time when talk of football lasted from late summer until after the bowl games on New Year's Day. Then there was the Super Bowl in late January or February. Then came the summer pre-season games, the Bowl Championship eliminations, the NFL/AFL playoffs, and the Divine Scorekeeper only knows what else. Nowadays there's hardly any such thing as a beginning or ending to football season.

There is Sunday Night Football, Monday Night Football and the occasional Tuesday Night Football...not to mention Thursday Night Football and Saturday Day and Night Football. The fact is that the diehard football fan can find a live or recorded game on TV at virtually any time of the day or night...any day or night of the year.

When I was a boy...and, for that matter, as I grew into young manhood...the family traditions were often scheduled around whatever football games were being televised. There we would sit with our TV trays of snacks, hunched forward to catch the action as it was projected on the screen of the one-eyed electronic idol.

When "the games" were on we would only grudgingly leave our spectator seats long enough to partake of the meal which was the excuse for the get-together, occasionally craning our necks to catch the action on the TV that was still blaring in the next room.

That doesn't happen as much these days. As the daddy to daughters, I inherited sons-in-law that weren't nearly so much absorbed by the broadcast sports...at least on these noteworthy family occasions...so the alternate cheering and jeering isn't heard nearly as often as it was in my youth.

I still watch the occasional game, though, and often feel that old excitement begins to stir as the two skilled teams square off against one another. It happened just the other day, in fact, as the "regular" season was making the transition into the "playoff" season.

It was an interesting game, even though the score was lopsided as a result of several unfortunate miscues by one of the teams. OK, they were really mismatched and outplayed.

There was an observation by one of the game's commentators that caught my attention as the second half was about to come to a close. He noted that even though the team with the ball was already ahead by a comfortable margin they automatically went into their "two-minute drill" as the clock wound down. He saw that as a sign of professionalism and discipline.

One doesn't have to be a rabid football fan to know about the two-minute drill. Simply put, it is a series of plays orchestrated to make efficient use of the short time that remains and designed to gain the maximum yardage, and, hopefully, a quick score.

The two-minute drill is a plan engineered with near mathematical skill, practiced repeatedly until it is imprinted permanently on the brains of the players, and perfected so that it will run flawlessly. That drill has been the salvation of many struggling teams in a game's closing minutes.

Have you ever asked yourself what you would do if you learned you only had a certain amount of time to live remaining? What... if anything...would you change about your life? Do you have a two-minute drill planned, and ready to put into action, just in case?

Here's another question for you: That idea of a two-minute drill is fine, but why should a team wait until time is about to run out to put that concentrated effort into the game? If each team played with that same dedication and effort every minute of the game, don't you think the outcome would be a lot better? And how much more is that true in our individual lives?

We can never be certain *which* two minutes will be our last, so it makes sense to me that we should strive daily to live with the same intensity as that two-minute drill, just to guarantee a win. Oh, and if you didn't already know it, our divine Coach, Jesus Christ, has already worked out that plan for you, if you'll only check with Him.

PARABLE OF THE PRETTY FACE

I know this will come as a shock to you, as it was to me, but a recent article about finding jobs in the current economic crisis led off with the statement, "Appearance has been shown to be an important factor in the hiring process." Well…duh.

I know, I know…the writer was probably a person raised in the generation of the politically correct, where we're all equal and everyone has a legal right to be protected from hurt feelings. And we are, after all, a society committed to the principle of equal opportunity and that anyone should have a fair chance at any job they find interesting.

A friend once shared some information with me and I responded, "Is that right?" His reply was, "It may not be *right*, but it's a fact."

The fact is that among all species I can think of…regardless of all other qualities a creature or thing may possess…appearance is virtually always an important factor in the selection process. The question is not whether or not this is a reality, but rather how heavily it should be weighed against those other qualities.

On a popular daytime TV show recently, a young man complained that he couldn't get a fair chance at a job…any job… because as a teen-ager he sought self-expression by "gauging" his ear lobes. That's where increasingly large disks are inserted in the pierced lobes, stretching them to the size of a silver dollar or larger. To him it was a creative statement. To potential employers it was a sign that he was weird…not a team player…would project a bad image. Right? Probably not, but his physical appearance was a factor they weren't willing to gamble on.

He was on the show because he wanted to have his lobes returned to their proper size, so his appearance would be more acceptable and encourage those companies to give him a chance to show that he could do the job they wanted done. Following the restoration of his "normal" ears, he applied for and got the job he desired.

Why are some people so surprised at this? Of course, it is superficial. Of course, it's not fair. But face it, folks, that's the way we're made. God created us as sensual people. We were intended to judge everything based on the way it looks, smells, sounds, tastes or feels. Those are the tools we were given, and man is going to use them in the common way.

God told Samuel, "Man looketh on the outward appearance…" It wasn't stated as a possibility or a personal preference, as if we had other choices, but as a fact of life. Right? No, but it's a fact.

It seems as if all of nature is a sucker for a "pretty face." The bright blossoms attract the bee. The colorful fruit attracts the birds and other creatures. The vibrant plumage entrances the female of the species.

God, on the other hand looks and sees things completely. His Word characterizes Him as evaluating not only the outward appearance, but the inner qualities and potential of His creation as well. In the first chapter of Genesis, we read over and over, at each stage of creation, "God saw…and it was good." Note that it doesn't say, "God saw…and it *looked* good."

Because we are created in His image, we can also look deeper than the pretty face, the handsome stature, if we are determined to do so. It takes some time…and patience…and a desire to know the person "behind the curtain" of looks, whether attractive or not. But we can do it.

I've written in the Parable of The Dumpster Diver how my wife, Lyn, was able to see beyond the "shelf appeal" of certain plants destined for the dumpster at the plant nursery where she worked. She would take those doomed plants with their drooping leaves and brown blossoms and somehow rehabilitate them. She developed a lovely garden of "foster" plants.

Just so, our loving Lord looks beneath the surface of each of us, and sees the true qualities that exist there, and determines how best to return us to beautiful, satisfying and productive life.

And you know what? His Spirit can teach each of us how to see beyond that first impression of a pretty—or not so pretty—face, and find a way to encourage and develop what dwells in the inner nature of each person with whom we come in contact.

❀

PARABLE OF THE BEST FRUIT

I love fresh fruit. I really like to start the day with whatever is in season. Half a grapefruit (especially the pink variety)—perhaps during the spring and summer a big wedge of cantaloup or honeydew melon—makes the perfect breakfast appetizer, in my book. Then during the week I'll usually slice some fresh strawberries and a handful of blueberries on a bowl of cereal for the main course. And, instead of milk I've learned to use a few dollops of plain yogurt. Just right!

We recently spent a week at our favorite Inn at the edge of the Smoky Mountains National Park, where the family-style breakfast and supper always include some type of fruit as a side dish. One day it might be pineapple chunks with grapes, on another perhaps cantaloup with a sprinkle of blueberries. Then there is one of the Inn's special dishes. They say the recipe for their Banana, Walnut and Honey dish is a family secret. Or is it?

Apples, oranges, grapes, peaches and pears in their season are among my favorite snacks in the afternoon. Sometimes they even take the place of the usual lunch.

Yes, I really love fresh fruit.

There's more to fruit than meets the palate, however. Not only is fruit "good, and good for you," but it also proves to be a fruitful source of illustrations.

For example, you've heard the expression, "Like comparing apples and oranges." Although they're both fruit, their natures are different, definitely not comparable.

Someone has observed that there are two types of religion...the "apple" type and the "orange" type. The orange, though containing the same color, texture and flavor throughout and surrounded by one continuous rind, is divided into a number of separate sections, each enclosed in its own protective membrane so it can't be touched or affected by the adjacent sections. Even the tiny juice cells within each section have their own protective cover. The only way to get the juice from an orange is to press it, mash it, and thereby break down the protective barriers separating the various elements, allowing the healthful juices to mix, blend and flow together. The pulp and the membranes offer texture and fiber, but add little to the flavor...in fact are often filtered out, leaving only the juice.

The apple, on the other hand, has all its juicy pulp together in one continuous whole, with every part sharing in the benefits of the apple tree's nutrients in equal parts. The very image of productive cooperation and community.

Churches...even individuals...in most denominations and religions can be said to fall into one of these two types. Sometimes they naturally mingle and form a continuous, nutritious whole. At other times the only way for them to become effective is to break down the artificial barriers that allow them to remain isolated in their own little cells, perhaps a number of cells cooperating among themselves, but not benefitting anyone or anything outside their "section," whether that be a Class, Small Group, or Department, Church or Denomination. We all know churches—and church members—like that, don't we? Once the peel is removed and the barriers are broken down, though, they are noteworthy for the good they can accomplish.

There's nothing wrong with being either an apple or an orange, as long as you remember that in order to be of any earthly good, you must climb out of the fruit bowl. Sometimes you'll need to offer yourself in bite-sized bits for the enrichment of those around you.

At other times your rind or peel has to be torn off or cut away...you may have to be broken, crushed, and pressed out in order to serve the purpose for which you were designed by the Divine Salad Chef.

And don't be surprised if those to whom you are served praise the Chef and not you, the fruit. That's the most positive assurance you can have that you have truly surrendered yourself to the preparation process of His will. Rejoice and be of good cheer...for He only serves the best.

PARABLE OF THE
BUSY WORK

Every parent has been there, I know. You have a chore to accomplish…it doesn't matter what it may be…and no sooner are you set up and ready to begin than one or more small voices pipe up in that earnest pleading, "Can I help?"

It makes no difference that they are disinterested in doing the simple daily chores that are their regular responsibility. That's no fun. When it's someone else's job they will fall all over themselves for the chance to help.

I think Mark Twain had it exactly right when he described Tom Sawyer enlisting…or rather "allowing"…the neighborhood boys to help whitewash Aunt Polly's fence. They even surrendered a wide variety of treasures for the privilege of wielding a paint brush.

When I was a boy, long before I was big enough to push the lawn mower myself, I was always eager to help Dad cut the grass. That was back in the day when few "civilians" had any kind of power mower. Like most folks, we had one of those reel-type push mowers that you seldom see outside a museum today. It was work to cut the grass in those days, and more than a boy my size could handle.

No matter. It looked like fun and I wanted some of it. I wanted to help. Dad called it my desire to "help him from working."

In order to encourage my occasional industrious enthusiasm, Dad would devise a multitude of little sub-chores requiring my particular expertise. He would delegate me to pick up sticks and twigs…or pine cones…or rocks. He would deputize me to bring us both a glass of ice water. In short, he would do his best to keep me occupied and out of his way while he completed his work. Dad said more than once that sometimes it was as difficult to think of enough "busy work" to keep me out from under foot as it was to perform the job he was intent on getting done.

When I adopted my "mostly" Black Lab companion Suzy Q Mahoney from Mostly Mutts, the animal rescue folks, they gave me some advice about how to walk her. They suggested that I get one of those saddle-bag type back-packs for her to wear. They have compartments to hold doggy treats, or water bottles…or even spare "puppy pooper" bags, if you like. I was told that this seems to give the dog a sense of purpose. I thought, "Sure. Whatever." So, I bought one.

I've tried it several times—although it's too hot for her during our summer walks—and you know what? It really works. She's a different pup when she is strapped into her little pink back-pack. Suzy isn't nearly so eager to start off to make friends—or a meal, I'm never quite sure which—of a nearby bird, squirrel or chipmunk. She is almost like a service dog.

Sensing that light burden on her back, she strides along as if on a mission, paying little attention to the usual distractions about her. Maybe I'm projecting, but it's as if that busy work gives her a sense of responsibility, a focus that she lacked before.

Have you ever thought that this is a lot like the way the Lord has to deal with "the people of His pasture…the sheep of His hand" (Psalm 95)?

Whether or not we, as His creatures, are aware of…and responsive to…Him as Creator and/or Friend, we go about our lives with a vengeance, striving to make things happen. We coax, cajole, wheedle and whack away, trying to shape events and circumstances the way we think they ought to be. We fearlessly jump in and "help"… much of the time getting in the way of the orderly progression of the Lord's work. He will often channel that enthusiasm into busy work.

The Lord's busy work for us is different in one respect, however. It is never wasted effort on our part. It always has a long-term benefit. But don't be surprised if your completed busy work seems to have little to do with what has finally been accomplished.

I am constantly amazed at what the Lord has done in my life, and in the lives of those I love, while I was engaged in whatever busy work I was assigned. Life has seemed like a much lighter burden since I learned to be content working on those things over which I could have some influence—my busy work—while leaving to Him those things that I could never control.

I have to go now…got some busy work to tend to.

PARABLE OF THE PEACEFUL RESISTANCE

There was an interesting bit of news tucked into the daily on-line reports recently that may not have caught your attention. I certainly didn't see anything about it on TV in the local or national reports of misery, doom and disaster.

Have you heard of DARPA, the Defense Advanced Research Project Agency? Did you know that they have developed an...I'm so old-fashioned I almost called it an airplane...a vehicle that is designed to fly at a speed of Mach 20. That's *twenty times the speed of sound!*

Not impressed? Let me put that into perspective for you. At the speed of Mach 20, one can fly from New York to Los Angeles in *twelve minutes.* A passenger would barely have time to tear open the package and eat the free peanuts before it was time to land. Of course, there would still be the two hours on either end to check for explosives and to wait for one's baggage.

As is the case with all such extraordinary developments, there is only one small glitch to be worked out before the airplay...I mean, the vehicle is ready for further testing. The Hypersonic Technology Vehicle (nicknamed the HTV-2...no indication of what happened to HTV-1) disappeared while on a test flight over the Pacific last August...just after reaching its maximum speed of Mach 20.

Here's the thing: Scientists believe that at that speed the vehicle simply flew out of its skin. No, really...the report stated they theorize that flying at twenty times the speed of sound can be bad for the skin. Especially if you're an HTV-2.

Just as the space shuttles use a protective ceramic heat shield to protect them during the high temperatures encountered upon re-entry into our atmosphere, the HTV-2 relied upon a protective skin. The only problem was that the skin of the craft encountered "impulsive shock waves" up to 100 times greater than they anticipated. And it just peeled off. Oops! Back to the drawing board.

Thomas Edison said after many attempts to produce artificial light that he didn't consider those efforts failures...he just said he had learned 10,000 ways *not* to make a lightbulb. Well...I suppose we could say that DARPA has learned one more way *not* to travel at Mach 20.

There's a reason why this news article caught my imagination. I had reminded someone just a few days before reading it that there are two Scripture verses that every Believer should keep in mind each day as they present their witness to the World. James wrote to his fellow Christians that they should 1) Submit themselves to God, and 2) Resist the devil and he will flee from them. One preacher said, "If you try to resist the devil without submitting yourself to God, the scoundrel will beat your britches!"

The other verse was from Paul's first letter to Timothy, where he cautioned him to flee the temptations and snares of the world. So, we are not to test our spiritual strength against temptation...we're to avoid it, to flee in the other direction. As evangelist Dr. Adrian Rogers said of the story of Joseph and Potiphar's wife, we should "saturate that place with our absence."

In our world today we tend to get those two bits of advice reversed. Look around you and notice how many have an almost superstitious fear of this spirit they call the devil. Yet they have no reluctance to toy with all manner of worldly temptations. "I can handle it," they tell themselves.

Face temptations, thinking you can resist them, and you'll eventually discover that the impulsive shock waves of the tempted life will peel away the protective skin of your spirit, and you will experience the same fate as good old HTV-2.

Peaceful resistance is good when applied in the proper order: 1) Flee temptation; 2) Submit yourself to God; *then* 3) Resist the devil and make *him* flee. That's the way to save your skin.

PARABLE OF THE JOLLY HOLIDAY

It's that time of year again—I don't know where the time has gone, do you? We have come crashing and stomping through another eleven months and it's time for the annual choosing up of sides for celebrating that most beloved holiday.

Don't puzzle too long over the "choosing up of sides" comment. You know what I mean...whether we'll call it Christmas or Winter Holiday...or even something more esoteric, like Winter Solstice. For a seasonal celebration that began as a more or less reverent observation of either a natural or supernatural event, it surely has been the source of a lot of angry rhetoric, hasn't it?

Most authorities seem to agree that the original observances of this season began when ancient tribes recognized the annual lowering of the sun toward the horizon and the shortening of daylight hours that accompanied it. As I searched for information on the subject, I found a web page that explained it this way:

"In pre-historic times, winter was a very difficult time for Aboriginal people in the northern latitudes. The growing season had ended and the tribe had to live off of stored food and whatever animals they could catch. The people would be troubled as the life-giving sun sank lower in the sky each noon. They feared that it would eventually disappear and leave them in permanent darkness and extreme cold. After the winter solstice, they would have reason to celebrate as they saw the sun rising and strengthening once more. Although many months of cold weather remained before spring, they took heart that the return of the warm season was inevitable. The concept of birth and or death/rebirth became associated with the winter solstice. The Aboriginal people had no elaborate instruments to detect the solstice. But they were able to notice a slight elevation of the sun's path within a few days after the solstice -- perhaps by DEC-25. Celebrations were often timed for about the 25th."

Many ancient peoples, from Egypt, Greece and Rome marked December 21 as a special day for feasting and celebration, often lasting for three days or more. In its determination to maintain control of conquered nations by exercising control over their religious practices, the Roman Empire, under Emperor Aurelian combined the solstice celebrations of the nativity of their various god-men/savior figures "into a single festival called the 'Birthday of the Unconquered Sun' on December 25th in about 275 CE."

Some of the religions with celebrations taking place at this time of the calendar year are Buddhism (Bodhi Day, the Sunday on or preceding December 8th); Christianity, of course (December 25th, with observations as early as the 4th Century AD); Druidism (at the Winter Solstice); Islam (Ramadan, lunar based and therefore not necessarily in December); Judaism (Hanukkah, or Festival of Lights, an eight-day observance occurring about the time of the Solstice); even Wicca and Vampires (not to be confused with the imaginary vampires of horror movie fame) have celebrations at the time of the Winter Solstice.

If you haven't dozed off during this riveting revelation of the history of this seasonal holiday, here's what I'd like to point out: During my lifetime I have observed an increasing sense of outrage and indignation among Christians and Christian churches at the attempts to secularize the Christmas holiday. In my view, many of these protesters miss the point completely.

Since the Romans, and later the early Christian Church... predominately, the Catholic Church...took advantage of existing pagan celebrations to establish the recognition of the birth of Jesus, there has been an increasing insistence that the world recognize the <u>Christ</u>mas season. Face it, folks...we hijacked *their* holiday, not the other way around.

Oops! I think I may have just gotten myself in trouble. Let me see if I can make my position clear before the torch-bearing mobs arrive with the tar and feathers.

How do the "Jesus is the reason for the season" adherents celebrate Christmas? They give presents—like pagans presented to their gods to persuade them not to take away the sun. They buy and decorate trees—the way ancient Druids did, I suppose, to help the Sun god find the entrance to the Underworld so he could enlighten it. They light candles—much as Jewish Hanukkah celebrants. And they...we...have borrowed other non-Christian customs to enrich our Christmas observances.

But these aren't the elements that make Christmas unique. And we shouldn't be surprised that unbelievers fail to understand that. Heck, even many church members don't.

True Christmas spirit begins in the heart. Should we give presents? Sure, in recognition of the priceless gift of Jesus, the sole Key to salvation from sin. Put up decorations? Of course, as an indication of the new life that is possible through trust in Him. Have parties and family gatherings? Certainly, as a means of sharing fellowship with other Believers and an opportunity to witness to those who are hopeless without Him in their lives.

However, I don't believe we do the cause of Christ any good when we become pugnacious and adversarial over what the season should be named...or how it should be celebrated. I had a professor of philosophy who once said, "You can't discuss color with one who is color-blind."

We can never expect the non-Christian world to understand or accept the significance of Christ in the affairs of mankind until they see it reflected in our lives, through our attitudes and actions. There's no point in trying to drag them, kicking and screaming, into our style of celebration. Even Jesus didn't do that.

But we can make it appealing by the joyful and loving way we live and serve each other and those around us. That is really the only way to make Christmas a truly jolly holiday. One that will last all year...every year...for a lifetime.

PARABLE OF THE SUCCESSFUL

Have you ever browsed the shelves of a well-stocked book store in the section usually identified with a sign such as "Success," "Self-Help," or "Motivational"? It is amazing to see all the varying views of what it is that constitutes "Success" and what it takes to achieve it.

There is a whole class of tomes on being successful that is based upon what the character Professor Harold Hill in the Broadway musical "The Music Man" called the "Think System." More accurately, I suppose, they are based upon an interpretation of a statement by the French philosopher René Descartes, "Cogito ergo sum," or, "I think, therefore I am."

Although Descartes was referring to the matter of man's existence, countless motivational speakers and writers...even fictional super-salesmen like Professor Hill...have expanded that thought to include the assertion that "Whatever you can think of, you can become." Or, as one writer put it, "You are not what you think you are...but what you THINK, you ARE." I just don't know about that, do you? Try thinking of yourself as a hippopotamus, and see if that works for you.

Anyway, following that logic, all one has to do to be successful is to think "successful thoughts." To visualize or picture oneself as being a success in whatever endeavor one wishes to undertake. This is also sometimes called the school of PMA...Positive Mental Attitude.

Some will maintain that the biggest obstacle to success is simply the failure to get started, the reluctance to take a risk. No one with the attitude of the old-time radio door-to-door salesman—who could be heard knocking on a door and muttering to himself, "Nobody home, I hope, I hope, I hope"—can ever hope to be successful. As all-time hockey great Wayne Gretzky once said, "You are *guaranteed* to miss 100% of the shots you don't take."

Other thinkers believe that success is determined by inspiration... some thought or insight that comes "out of the blue," which, if acted upon, will lead the way to success. That seems a little whimsical, doesn't it? To think that all one has to do to be successful is be at the right place at the right time and wait patiently until something...or someone..."inspirates" him? All those that show up at the wrong place and time are doomed? Does that seem fair?

Besides...Thomas Edison insisted that Success is "Five percent Inspiration and Ninety-five percent Perspiration." But lest we begin to think that hard work alone is the answer to success, remember the definition of a fanatic: One who, when he loses sight of his goal, redoubles his efforts.

Hard work certainly does play a part in every success, of course. Often, like boys wrestling on a hillside, playing "One Man Stands," the one who is strongest and holds out the longest will be the one who wins the game. A famous football coach-turned-motivational-speaker once said that the five most important words are "Never, never, never, never QUIT!"

However, hard work in itself doesn't always guarantee success either. I once saw a motto that read "If at first you don't succeed... you're just about average." I also came across this humorous parody of a famous Edgar A. Guest poem, "So I tackled the thing that 'couldn't be done'...and I couldn't do it either." And there's always this advice to the unsuccessful: "When all else fails, pitch a fit."?

How about thoughtful goal-setting? Is that the key to Success? Should we take seriously the sign over the doughnut machine that read "As on through life you travel, whate'er may be your goal, Keep your eye upon the doughnut, And not upon the hole."?

If this were a test, "What is it that makes one successful?" would have to be a multiple-choice question. And one of the choices would have to be "All of the above." The recipe for success, like any other recipe in Mom's cookbook, has many ingredients. Each is important, introduced at the proper time and proper amount to achieve the desired result.

We've already mentioned most of the "-tions" that are essential ingredients for what most folks call success: Inspira*tion*, Motiva*tion*, Prepara*tion*, Execu*tion*, Perspira*tion*. However, there's a question we haven't yet considered.

I've written before that one of the saddest realizations in life is to have struggled up the so-called Ladder of Success...only to find that it's leaning against the wrong wall. So many successfully achieve their goals, only to find the success unsatisfying and hollow, and to discover they didn't even enjoy the climb.

For those who will be faithful, the Bible promises "Seek ye first the Kingdom of God and His righteousness, and all these things will be added unto you." (Matthew 6:33) Success...as the Lord defines it... is to be found in applying all the ingredients we've mentioned, in pursuit of His Will for our lives.

Among my favorite Scripture passages are these verses from Psalms 37: "Delight thyself also in the Lord, and He shall give thee the desires of thine heart. Commit thy way unto the Lord; trust also in Him, and He shall bring it to pass." In Jack's paraphrase: He will

reveal what your heart should desire, and then provide it to you. So turn your handlebars over to the Lord and leave the steering to Him. You'll still have to do the peddling, but your destination is assured.

That is the Success promised to each Believer. Are you on the road to Success?

PARABLE OF THE COMFORTABLE CALL

From the time I was a little boy it was assumed that I would go to Georgia Tech. I remember Mom teaching me the words to the Tech fight song–The Rambling Wreck–when I was only six or seven years old. "I'm a ram-bling wreck from Geor-gia Tech, and a heck-of-an en-gin-eer..." At least that's the way I learned it at that age.

I'm not sure why Mom and Dad were such Tech fans. I'm not aware of any of my direct relatives that went to college...maybe some cousins a time or two removed, and a great uncle or so...but I'm not certain. Although Dad was one of the wisest and most intelligent people I've ever known, he dropped out of the eighth grade so he could get a job to help support the family.

I remember my mom telling me, "You like to draw, and you like to put things together. I think you need to go to Georgia Tech and study to be an Architectural Engineer." So, I grew up assuming that was what I would do.

All the way through high school I took the College Prep curriculum. I was in the top third of my class...things seemed to be going according to plan. Until the Spring of my Junior year, when I came crashing up against reality.

I don't know how things work in high school these days, but back then that was the time in one's high school career when planning for college and career became serious. I spent a lot of time with my counselor, Mr. Bill Bryce, and took a whole battery of tests to help map out a life strategy.

One of the tests I recall was the Cuder Preference Test. I'm told they still use a version of that test today. It measures one's likes and dislikes...one's preferences...and points to areas where one is most likely to be successful, on the premise that our preferences generally follow along the lines of our innate abilities.

I remember sitting across the desk from Mr. Bryce, reviewing the results of my tests, and hearing him say, "So, you really want to go to Tech? Your tests and grades tell me that engineering is not your strong suit. If you're determined to go to Georgia Tech, I suggest you study Industrial Management (that's what they called their management major in those days). That will give you a broad education in a lot of areas and give you good preparation for whatever kind of business you eventually get into."

So...I wasn't going to be an Architectural Engineer...whatever that is...after all. Bummer. But at least I was still qualified to attend Georgia Tech, even if only as an Industrial Management major. I remember at Freshman orientation, one of my fellow "rats" remarking, "Why in the world would you *start out* as an IM? What are you going to *drop back* to?" I felt better, though, when someone pointed out that it was most often the IM's that hired and fired the Engineers.

I'll say this for my Georgia Tech education: I learned that as important as it is to learn and master a body of facts, it is vastly more important to learn how to find and evaluate facts mastered and recorded by others. In other words, it taught me how to learn. A very valuable skill, indeed.

When Pastor Craig Harwood preached a sermon about his being called into areas where he felt unqualified and incapable of dealing with, he asserted, "God will probably not call one to serve in a place where he feels fully qualified and capable, because it would be only natural for that one to rely upon his own skills and wisdom. The Lord usually places us in positions where we must depend upon Him, His power and inspiration."

I can't tell you how many times since I left Tech with that seemingly all-important diploma in hand that I have found myself in situations where I asked myself, "What am I doing here? What do I do now?" That piece of sheepskin didn't come with instructions...no owner's manual or GPS.

Have you ever felt that way? Ever asked yourself how you were going to deal with some new, strange situation? I have. I've felt like that candidate for the Vice Presidency years ago, who began his speech by saying, "What is my name? Why am I here?"

Whenever you are tempted to feel incapable and inadequate, my dad had a saying that you should keep in mind. He said, "The only ability that the Lord requires is AVAIL-ability." He never puts us in a position where He cannot use us to work His will. All He expects of us is to show up.

If you doubt that, just check out the Life Manual...the Bible. Almost without exception, whenever He called someone to a task, the individual protested his lack of ability, skill or opportunity. That didn't discourage the Lord, He used them anyway...and the result was always some kind of great and mighty work.

So, stop hoping and praying for some sort of Comfortable Call. Be available...ready to do great things. But don't be surprised if He leads you to do small things in a great way...a way that suits His will for you. And then, simply leave the results to Him.

PARABLE OF THE BUSINESS OF THE BLOSSOM

I heard a report the other day that informed us that this has been the warmest winter since scientists and "weather guessers" have been keeping track. Of course, they didn't have the ability to keep track, or to collect and coordinate information from around the world until the late 1800's, but, still, that covers a period of 120 or 130 years.

Aside from giving the global warming and climate change "doom and gloomers" fodder for their dire prognostications, the unseasonably warm winter has caused those plants, trees and shrubs that generally make up the welcoming committee that heralds the approach of Spring to break out their banners of blossoms sooner than usual. A landscaper friend of mine put it this way, "Yep, everything's blooming about three to four weeks early this year."

I don't know, but it seems that every year we discuss whether the dogwoods and azaleas will be at their glorious best for Easter weekend. Some years they make it...some years not. This was a "not" year...by Easter most of the trees and shrubs had, as one of my young friends once said, begun to "drop their bloomers."

That revelation struck me most forcibly the other morning as my mostly black Lab, Suzy Q Mahoney, and I were taking our morning necessary walk. Everywhere we walked, the path was strewn with the petals of dogwood, redbud, wild cherry, flowering crab...if it had blossoms, they were strewn. With all those flowers spread on our way, looking for all the world like preparation for the passing of royalty...or at least a rock star...I felt like waving and saying, "Oh, you shouldn't have gone to all this trouble just for Suzy and me...but we're glad you did. Thank you."

As we continued on our rounds, treading lightly on the petal-dappled pavement, I felt just a touch of melancholy over the transition of the brightly colored branches to the more practical and long-lasting green foliage that would sustain life through Spring and Summer. "Well," I thought, "at least the pretty blossoms have served their purpose."

Served their purpose. Have you ever thought exactly what *is* the purpose of those exquisite flowers and blossoms we admire and treasure so greatly? As one beautiful movie star was heard to complain, "I'm more than just a pretty face, you know."

Scientists, not always noted for their romantic point of view, tell us that the blossom of each species of plant is nothing more than a shameless advertisement designed to attract attention. The color, size, shape, and even its location on the plant, are intended to attract specific customers to help pollinate and propagate itself...to fertilize the fruit which will generate and protect the seed which will, in turn, insure the continuation of the species.

After the colorful blossom has attracted the honey bee or wasp... or whatever flying or creeping thing will best serve the purposes of procreation...it has served its purpose, and, in the economy of botanical systems, withers away and is carried off by wind and gravity to be returned to the soil. Its nutrients are recycled and prepared for next year's gala presentation of glory.

The same can be said for every kind of physical beauty, can't it? At first, there is the experience of joy at the sight of something lovely.

Then there is a selection of the most pleasing of those attractive things. From then on appearance becomes secondary...the utility and ability to serve a purpose is what counts. And that's true whether we're talking about things or people, isn't it?

The Lord gave us the ability to appreciate a pleasing appearance and the urge to make a selection based upon that outward attraction. He also gave us wisdom to appreciate the inner qualities that give that thing...or that person...real value to us as we go about the tasks of living full and meaningful lives. You'll never be satisfied if you try to enjoy one without the other.

PARABLE OF THE SOFT ROCK THEORY

No, this isn't going to be a discussion of my ideas about today's music preferences. I've written about those before, and probably will again, but not this time. Instead, I want to share a thought that has been lounging around in the back room of my mind for a couple of weeks, waiting for the right time to step into my conscious and trickle through my fingertips onto the keyboard.

It occurred to me that there are few activities as restful and relaxing as simply sitting in a nice, comfortable rocking chair and gently rocking back and forth, forward and backward, while all the world around me goes spinning helter-skelter in frantic orbit.

As my Joyce and I go walking through our neighborhood it is interesting to notice all the houses with front porches. There was a time—I suppose that it was before every house had air-conditioning and large-screen, high-definition television—when whole families would collect on those porches and sit in their rocking chairs and porch swings, engaging in relaxed conversation, reading, or perhaps sharing a word of greeting with neighbors and the occasional passerby.

One doesn't see that much these days. Oh, the rockers and swings are still prominent fixtures on the porches, only you seldom see anyone using them. It's too hot...or too cold...or too still...or too windy. And, besides, who has time to just sit and rock or swing anymore?

When one stops to think about it, though, there's more to rocking than simply resting and relaxing. Have you ever paid attention to a mother or father trying to soothe a fretful baby? They will pat, they will hum or sing, they will bounce; but the one thing that works most is simply to rock gently back and forth. That usually does the trick, doesn't it?

The other day my Joyce brought home a *Woman's World* magazine from the grocery store—she *never* brings magazines home from the grocery store—with some articles that had caught her eye. They were about how to have "the best summer ever," or something like that. One of the suggestions that brought my lounging thoughts onto my mental front porch was a brief item titled "Rock Yourself Calm."

The article recommended taking a break in a rocking chair or hammock as an easy way to relieve stress. It quoted a University of Rochester study which found that "the more anxiety-prone adults gently rocked back and forth, the calmer they became." It went on to say that "the soothing rhythmic motion of rocking spurs your brain to produce endorphins, the 'happy' chemicals that ease stress and boost your mood."

Further, the article endorses slowly rocking in a rocker before getting into bed as a stress relieving sleep aid. The article closes by saying that a study reported in the journal *Cell Biology* indicates that gentle rocking helps one more quickly "reach the deepest and most restorative stages of sleep." I don't know about you, but I've had a few nights when that would have helped.

Yes, there are few activities as calming and relaxing as a short rock in one of our Jumbo Porch Rockers, made right here in town, or a slow, gentle swing in our Pawleys Island rope hammock, made at our favorite beach in South Carolina. And it doesn't take long at all for the tension and troubling thoughts of the moment to simply drift away.

However, there is another side to the theory of the soft rock and the soothing swing. There always comes the time to get out of that comforting rocking chair and that peaceful hammock, and get back to the business of life. No matter how peaceful the "time out," the responsibilities and opportunities of the day constantly beckon, and must be attended.

As one back porch philosopher put it, "No matter how much energy and effort you put into that rocking chair, you still have to get out of it or you'll never get anywhere." A purposeful rock, or a satisfying swing can, indeed, provide a "pause that refreshes," as the familiar soft drink slogan promises, but there always comes the time to get up and go back to the work of living.

After the mighty work of creating the entire universe, decorating it, populating it, and then putting it into motion, Almighty God set the example for all mankind to follow through the ages. He portioned off one seventh of what we call "Time" and designated that as a regular period for rest.

It is good for each of us to engage in some sort of work, or purposeful activity that is worth doing; to carry out our responsibilities, to take advantage of opportunities for service to others...and to do these things with energy and determination. Then, however, it's time for some restful rocking...some soothing swinging...to get our physical and mental tempos back in rhythm.

And what about those times of tension and stress when you don't have a rocking chair or a porch swing, or a hammock handy? Just sit down, close your eyes, and slowly rock back and forth as you imagine yourself sitting in the lap of God while He rocks you, His much-loved child, and eases away the cares of this world.

Then, get up and get back to the work of serving Him with renewed energy and faith. The Lord will still have those soft, spiritual rockers, swings and hammocks there when you need them.

And that's not just a theory. It's a fact you can count on.

PARABLE OF THE
GUILTY PARTY

If you've read many of these Parables, you're already aware that I have always been a great fan of the comic strips. Some of the most profound wisdom and commentary I've ever discovered in print can be found in what we used to call the "Funny Papers."

My list of favorites is quite large, and it varies from time to time, depending upon the publication I happen to be reading, but there are several that are consistently at the top of the list. "Pogo" by Walt Kelly..."Li'l Abner" by Al Capp..."BC" and "Wizard of Id" by Johnny Hart..."Peanuts" by Charles Schultz..."Calvin and Hobbes" by Bill Waterson are all dear to my heart, although no longer in current production.

Another strip I have appreciated over the years is "Family Circus" by Bill Keane. In his biographical sketch, Keane says he was born in Philadelphia, home of Benjamin Franklin and the Liberty Bell. When he was a boy seeing the Liberty Bell for the first time, someone reflected idly, "Who cracked the Liberty Bell?" Keane said he responded, "Not me." That later became the name of one of the imaginary culprits in Family Circus. The other one was "Ida Know."

Anyone who has reared children...or spent any amount of time with them, for that matter...has noticed that when bad things happen "it's not my fault." They'll take credit for anything with a good result, but never when things go wrong. The guilty party is usually Not Me or Ida Know.

And, of course, children aren't the only ones quick to dodge blame for unpleasant or unexpected outcomes. Adults are the undisputed leaders in passing the buck when things go wrong. Even when backed into a corner, with irrefutable evidence of guilt, the accused party can find a way to avoid accepting the full blame.

Just observe the daily news for a few minutes and you'll accumulate a list of dozens of excuses for bad behavior. Temporary insanity...childhood abuse...bullying...global warming...stockholder greed...bipolar disorder...post-traumatic stress syndrome...faulty brakes or accelerators. Of course, there are circumstances when these are legitimate reasons for people's actions. However, there are multitudes of cases where they're simply excuses. Nothing more.

Countless guilty parties will latch onto one of them to justify themselves. The News at Eleven is packed with reports of everyone from politicians to pickpockets...perverts to power brokers...who will, when caught in some crime or misdemeanor, find a way to point the finger at Not Me or Ida Know. It's never their fault...at least, not completely. There's always someone else to blame.

I've noticed that we seem to be so conditioned to avoid taking credit for our failings that we often also unconsciously resist compliments for good deeds. What I have heard called the "Aw, shucks" Syndrome is just a way to avoid the "blame" for doing something thoughtful or exemplary.

In John 5:1-18, we read the story of the lame man at the pool of Bethesda and his encounter with Jesus. He had been lying there for thirty-eight years awaiting the legendary stirring of the waters, supposed to bring healing to the first party to enter the pool.

Jesus asked him, "Do you want to be made well?" Instead of answering the Lord's question, he gave an excuse for not already being well. "There's nobody to help me into the pool," he said, "It's not my fault." Jesus didn't bother arguing with him, He just told him to get up, take his pallet and go home. His body was healed.

Later, when the Pharisees accused the man of breaking the Sabbath laws by carrying his pallet, he said, "It's not my fault. The man who healed me told me to do it." Not Me strikes again.

I find it interesting that Jesus sought him out and told him, "See, you have been made well. Sin no more lest a worse thing come upon you." (NKJV) Sin no more?

Maybe it's because I had been thinking about this tendency, we all have to avoid blame...pass the buck...make excuses, that it occurred to me that perhaps the Lord wasn't just referring to some generic idea of sin. Could it be that He was saying that the failure to take responsibility for our actions is some kind of sin?

Scholars in Greek and Aramaic, and experienced commentators on the Bible will probably disagree with this particular interpretation, but I have experienced the way the Spirit uses the living Scriptures to communicate a multitude of messages to faithful readers. And this is what the Spirit has led me to in this particular passage on this particular day.

It's not a very big stretch for me to think of dodging the guilt for my own actions as a degree of sin. After all, as far as I can tell, the lame man didn't sin by lying there at the pool for thirty-eight years. His sin seems to be in blaming his own inaction...or ability to act...on the absence of help from others. In Jesus' eyes, he didn't sin by carrying his pallet on the Sabbath, but by not accepting the responsibility for his actions before the Pharisees.

The murderer...the sexual predator...the drug addict...the thief... the liar...the cheat...the swindler. They are all sinners in their own ways, but I believe that they also sin—and, in many cases society supports them—by attempting to place the blame, shame and guilt upon someone else.

One thing is certain. When we stand before the Judgment Throne, neither Not Me nor Ida Know will be acceptable defenses. For we are all without excuse, and Jesus is our only defense.

PARABLE OF THE ANATOMY OF A WITNESS

I received a summons the other day. It's not what you might think; it was a summons to Jury Duty. I've been summoned a number of times before...and occasionally been selected to serve on a jury panel. Most of the time, however, I was released after a few hours in the Jurors' waiting room.

The constitution provides that each person accused of a crime is entitled to be judged by a "jury of his, or her, peers." I've learned that this doesn't necessarily mean that the jury will be made up of people just like the defendant, but that each attorney will select from the jury pool those he believes to be the best to support his side of the case.

I don't know if it's the manner of my dress, my white hair, or my sincere countenance that makes the difference, but, even when my particular pool is called into the courtroom, I'm usually stricken by one side or the other. And, to be honest with you, that doesn't hurt my feelings.

I have to admit, however, that the few cases for which I have been selected have been very interesting and informative. Especially for anyone who has grown up with the likes of TV's Perry Mason, LA Law, Boston Legal, and even Judge Judy. To be as realistic as those shows have seemed, it's amazing to see that they are hardly anything like real life. There's very little drama to the usual case...no startling revelations...last minute confessions from the witness stand...stirring closing arguments.

There is one aspect of the typical trial that I find interesting, though, and that is the questioning and testimony of the various witnesses...whether for the plaintiff or the defendant. They are only allowed to give testimony about facts or events which they have personally known or experienced. Anything else is inadmissible as "hearsay evidence," or as relating to "facts not in evidence." Any fan of the TV courtroom shows knows that.

In short, then, a witness is only called to the stand if he or she has personal knowledge or information or facts that relate directly to the arguments of the defense or prosecution of the case. The task of the jury is to discern whether those facts reflect the guilt or innocence of the accused.

It occurred to me that those rules also apply to the realities of our daily lives. We are continually expected to give testimony to our personal knowledge and experience with various aspects of life. And we are likewise cautioned to carefully evaluate the assertions and actions of others to determine whether they are valid, true and dependable.

In Acts 1:8 we read, "...you *will* be witnesses to Me..." (Emphasis added). Just as surely as if we were summoned to serve in a courtroom, we are...by our nature as Believers...constantly on the witness stand. Our lives themselves serve as silent...or not so silent...testimony to what the Lord has done in us. We can't help or avoid it. The world is observing us wherever we go, and in whatever endeavors we are engaged.

Unfortunately, however, there are many members of Christian churches and organizations who have not had a personal experience with Jesus, and are consequently guilty of offering hearsay evidence. The world judges the Church harshly because of that false testimony.

The Church is not totally innocent, either, because in its eagerness to bring in and minister to the lost there is quite often a failure to develop and disciple them in the Word...to lead them into that personal relationship with the Lord whereby they concede control of their lives to Him. Then, and only then, is their witness likely to be effective in leading others into a similar relationship.

You might be tempted to say, "It's not for us to judge," but you would be wrong...and out of step with the Scriptures. As Believers, we are to serve as jurors, discerning facts that indicate the guilt or innocence of the accused. Otherwise, how can we minister to them and lead them into that relationship with the Lord? So...have you witnessed, or exercised discernment today? Why not?

PARABLE OF THE HEARING EAR

I t hasn't been too many years since CB radios were all the rage among those who spent a lot of time on the road. I understand they are still in common use among truckers and long-haul drivers, but I suppose the cell phone has taken over in popularity these days. Hands free, or Blue-tooth (whatever that is), of course.

When CBs were the fad, though, there was a jargon that became popular among users as a kind of verbal shorthand. One of the phrases that I recall was "Got your ears on?" It was usually directed at a specific individual, and meant, "Are you there? Is your radio on? Are you listening for what I have to say?"

That always seemed a little silly to me, because if the party wasn't tuned in...well, he wouldn't even hear the question, would he? But the question still has an application in ordinary, everyday conversation, I think.

It's obvious that we all have ears. God designed each of us with one hung on either side of our heads, turned so we could receive sound in stereo and determine the direction from which it comes. They funnel those vibrations through a series of filters and amplifiers to the brain, where they are analyzed, evaluated and identified so we can respond to the information they bear.

Yes, we all have ears, but, as any wife or mother will tell you we can hear without listening...without our brains absorbing the significance of what our ears perceive. And it isn't only husbands and small children who are guilty. In fact, without the capacity of "selective hearing"...the ability to sub-consciously filter out unimportant or unwanted sounds, whether noise or conversation...rational thought and action would be extremely difficult. Ask any parent.

My Dad came home from his two years in the Navy with a phrase he used frequently around the house. "Now hear this!" he would say, before making some significant pronouncement or giving important instructions. That was the way the ship's skipper got the attention of all hands when broadcasting over the ship's communication system. It meant, "Listen up, pay attention to what I'm saying...and then obey."

In these days when we have progressed from the Walkman to the iPod...from headphones to ear-buds...from background music to bone-crushing, ear-splitting hard rock, it's an easy matter to block out or overwhelm sounds you aren't interested in hearing. In fact, it's often necessary to physically get the attention of someone before engaging them in conversation.

There are approximately 1,000 times in the King James Version where the writers use words translated "Hear" or some variation of it. I haven't counted, but I suspect there are very few of those instances where the mere passive receipt of sound vibrations is what is meant by the text.

When the Psalmist sings out at the top of his voice, "Hear me, Lord!" he's not asking if the Lord has His ears on. He's praying for the Lord's attention...for His understanding of what is in his heart...for His intervention, and action on his behalf.

When the Old Testament priests proclaimed, "Hear, O Israel! The Lord our God is one God," they weren't merely implying that the people should learn the words so they could be repeated in ritualistic fashion. They were admonishing them to accept and respond to the reality of the power and righteous rule of Almighty God.

When Jesus says, "Those who have ears to hear, let them hear," He means for all who wish to follow Him to listen...pay attention... and then obey.

Like the man in the cell phone commercial on TV, the Spirit constantly asks, "Can you hear me now?" And we don't truly hear Him unless we are prepared to *do* something about what we hear.

PARABLE OF THE PAYMENT PLAN

My Dad wasn't always a wily shopper, but when he set his mind to it he could be. Over the years I got the impression that he might have been overcompensating for his experiences during the difficult times of the Great Depression.

Many are the times when considering a purchase...whether for himself or for one of the family members...he would tell my sisters and me, "For a little bit more you can go First Class." That was certainly not the way he was reared, however.

Like most of those who had struggled through tough economic challenges, my grandmother, Ma-Ma, approached shopping as if it were a contact sport. She took each trip to the store...any store, for any purchase...with the seriousness of a battle commander planning a campaign. She was the ultimate frugal—some might label her "cheap"—shopper.

At Rich's Department Store...for the better part of a century *the* place to buy everything from baby shoes to full-length furs, from frying pans to automobile tires...Ma-Ma would go through an entire counter of articles, examining every seam, button and zipper, looking for imperfections and flaws that she could use to get a little off the ticket price. And she always found something.

Ma-Ma almost never bought something that was in the current style. She always waited until the season changed and things went on sale. She bought Christmas gifts in January and warehoused them in her cedar chest until time to wrap them up for seasonal giving. My sisters and I took delight in sniffing the gifts under the Christmas tree to identify those from Ma-Ma. They almost always had the telltale scent of cedar.

I never knew if Dad found these shopping habits of his mother to be quaint or embarrassing. I do know he teased her a lot about them, though. And most of the time he went to the other extreme. On ordinary purchases he seldom even asked the price, and never bargained or haggled.

About the only time I remember Dad dusting off the skills he had learned from Ma-Ma was when he asked a salesman, "Ninety days same as cash?" He would often agree to pay three payments...30, 60 and 90 days...with no interest added to the price.

I recently had some home improvements done, and, almost as a reflex, I asked, "Ninety days same as cash?" The salesman said, "I can do better than that. How about *twelve months* same as cash?" He then told me that there would be a regular loan agreement, but that as long as I made the regular payments on time there would be no interest charges. I could live with that payment plan

I thought about that payment plan a while back as I read the story of Moses, Aaron and the incident of the Golden Calf. You remember the story: Moses on the mountain with God, receiving the Ten Commandments; poor old weak-willed Aaron trying to keep the people under control in Moses' absence, agreeing to make a "God substitute" out of their gold jewelry...a Golden Calf.

I had most of the story clearly in mind, with Moses breaking the stone tablets in his anger with the Israelites, and God threatening to destroy the people and start all over again with Moses and his offspring. I remembered Moses pleading the case for the Israelites and coaxing the Lord to give them another chance.

There's one small part of the story that I didn't recall, however. Although God relented and put aside His anger, the Bible quotes, "... when the time comes for me to punish, I will punish them for their sin." Why should it come as a surprise to us that there is a definite payment plan for sin?

When we're tempted to ask with the Psalmist why the wicked prosper, we simply need to remember that they, too, are on a payment plan. The only difference for Believers is that when the time for our final payment arrives our agreement is marked "Paid," and signed by Jesus.

PARABLE OF THE DEVILED EGG

I came to the manly art of cooking late in life...and, as I have revealed before, I didn't come to it naturally. My Dad's philosophy was that he was good at what he got paid for and he was willing to pay others to do what they were good at...including cooking.

I've also written that Dad's idea of cooking for himself was heating a can of Gebhardt's Chili con Carne in a pot of boiling water and eating it from the can. One pot...one fork...toss the can...no muss, no fuss, no bother. No, although Dad was my ideal...my shining example in many things, those things didn't include the culinary arts.

As a boy I remember spending many hours watching Mom preparing our meals...never anything elegant, just plain Southern home cooking. I never realized until I began cooking for myself how much of that experience I had retained.

Actually, now that I think about it, my earliest efforts in the kitchen began as a short-order cook when our family took our annual trip with our friends the Willieses to the Sawyer-Davis cottage on Pawleys Island, South Carolina. Mac and I would alternate preparing breakfast for our two families. Even now, whenever the family goes to Pawleys, breakfast is my responsibility.

As I have gradually expanded my cooking expertise, I've found that once I get past the menu planning stage it can be a lot of fun. And, as I told someone recently, I enjoy my own cooking enough that I'm not wasting away...or waisting away, either.

Don't get me wrong. If I were to compile all my knowledge and skill in the kitchen, along with all the recipes and menus I have mastered, and put it all into a book...perhaps titled "Observations of Foo Foo the Chef"...it would be only a small pamphlet at best. But I'm learning.

I climbed aboard this train of thought while trying to decide what offering I would bring to the next family gathering. Most of the easy things were taken. I was going to pick up one of those spiral-sliced hams...quick, easy, and worthy of Dad's example. But no, someone else beat me to it.

Then I thought, "What about deviled eggs? I think I remember how Mom made those...and they were always a hit." Just to be sure that was something I could reasonably expect to do, I went on-line (Isn't that interesting? Lyn had four bookshelves of cookbooks and a foot high stack of file folders containing recipes she had accumulated during 50 years of cooking for the family. Yet I went on-line to find a recipe.) to see what I could find.

Who knew that there is an entire science that has developed around the art of properly boiling an egg? After all, you don't want the yolk to be runny...or dry and mealy...or have that mysterious-looking green coating...or smell sulphureous, do you? Of course not. So, follow the rules.

And boiling the egg...even when applying the most advanced scientific techniques...is the easiest part. One doesn't merely scoop out the yolks, mix in some stuff and put them back. Oh, no. Even Dad could do that. No...you must use "special" stuff, and measure, and mix...and one can even find special apparatus to do deviled eggs properly.

As I looked over the detailed instructions and planned my attack, a peculiar question came to mind: Where did the name "deviled eggs" come from? And my mind raced off on another rabbit trail. Of Course, that's where a lot of these Parables originate.

Dieticians tell us that the "incredible, edible egg" is an excellent source of protein and other important nutrients. An egg or two a day can be the basis for a very healthy diet. It's what we add to it...and how we prepare it...and how many we eat...that has given the egg its bad reputation.

Take the yolks of eggs, add a little mayonnaise, a little mustard, salt and pepper...oh, and some sweet pickle relish, and minced olives... garlic powder...a dash of cayenne pepper...chopped tarragon... Mix it all thoroughly until smooth and creamy and, using one of those cake decorating tube thingys, squeeze the mixture into the waiting whites. Perhaps a little paprika or some garnish on top for looks. There you have a delicious and appealing masterpiece. No longer just "eggs".

Isn't that just the way the adversary works? In case you haven't noticed, he always begins his persuasions with something that is good and turns it into something he can use to lead us astray. He takes simple, uncomplicated concepts and adds embellishments that soon overwhelm the original ideas, taking away anything good and useful and making them difficult and burdensome.

God wants His people to be joyful and productive. The adversary cannot abide a joyful spirit and all of his efforts are aimed at disturbing our sense of peace. He rebukes us with "Stop enjoying your life, this is supposed to be work, not fun."

So...enjoy your day today. Add all the little things that bring you joy...but don't let it become a "deviled egg" day, so full of the drudgery of preparation and extraneous ingredients that it becomes harmful to you both in body and in spirit.

PARABLE OF THE EMPTY HOUSE

During the ten years I spent in Miss Connie's Sunday School class, sitting in the floor with the three-year-old's, I heard her make the comment a number of times. On the first occasion she said it I recall thinking, "That's an unusual thing to talk about around children this age, but I think she's right." It all started with a realtor's sign she drove past that read "Home for Sale."

"You can't sell a home," she complained. "A home is what's made up of the family that lives *inside* the house. You can sell the house, but you can't sell the home."

Although I'd never thought about it in exactly those terms, I agreed with her completely. A home is a living, breathing entity, a group of individuals, bonded together with common goals and interests, dwelling within the physical structure we call a house. Families...homes...can come and go, but the house remains where it is until it's torn down or falls in on itself.

This experience came to mind the other day during a discussion with a friend who was recently widowed. While dealing with her own grief, she described the pain and difficulty of trying to answer the questions of her small grandson about where "Paw-paw" was...about his death, and why it was a good thing that he was now "in Heaven."

The little boy had seen the handsomely appointed coffin, and the flowers...heard the loving comments of friends and visitors about the grandfather he loved...listened to the music and prayers during the memorial observance for this special person in his life. Then, he went with the family to the graveside service, where all these events came into focus.

"Paw-paw's going in there?!" he wailed, pointing to the open grave as the coffin was lowered into its resting place. A bewildering, horrifying thought for one so young.

How do you explain the mysteries of life and death to one who experiences loss for the first time...or, for that matter, even to those who have experienced it over and over?

My grandfather heart began to think of ways to ease the tortured thoughts of one who has no concept of the realities of death, or heaven...perhaps without even a clear understanding of the wisdom and nature of a just and loving God, and His perfect plan for each of those who are His.

I thought about my dad, who donated his body to the Emory University School of Medicine, and said, more than once, "When I die, I'm going to be with the Lord. My body is just the empty husk I'll leave behind. It might as well be put to some useful purpose, even if it's only for parts." The body is merely the husk, no longer required as a container for the life that once resided there.

I thought about the illustration of a scented candle. You bring life to a candle by lighting it, and that light brightens the room... the fragrance permeates the space around it, touching the senses of everyone nearby. When the flame is extinguished, the fragrance remains for a long time...the candle can be left where it is or stored in a drawer until the next time it is needed. The physical candle was merely the storage place from which the light and aroma originated.

As I pondered that question, the Spirit gently pushed my Replay button and positioned my mental cursor over the file containing Miss Connie's comment about houses and homes. And there, I believe, highlighted a more suitable illustration to soothe the hurt feelings of those beset by grief.

Each of us is born, as the Bible expresses it, a living soul. That soul is the spiritual essence, the personality that makes each of us an individual...the collection of qualities that gives each person a distinct nature.

That soul...that family of qualities...that spirit "home"...is then placed into a physical structure we identify and recognize as our "house"...our body, with all its abilities and attributes that serve us as we proceed through our daily existence and have our influence upon the lives of those who are near and dear to us.

That body...that house, if you will...grows and develops. It gets added onto and remodeled, redecorated and redesigned. And, eventually, it becomes worn out and unable to meet our needs any longer. That's the way houses are made, you know...planned as more or less temporary dwelling places to meet specific needs for a specific period of time.

When the physical house no longer serves its purpose as a residence, eventually the family...the home...moves to a better one somewhere else. Likewise, the soul's house may be left empty, to be torn down, its rubble buried; although the soul home that once resided there continues forever, relocated to its eternal dwelling place.

That's why I no longer have any dread about eventually moving out of this house that I've lived in for all these years. In the words of a favorite gospel song that I've sung often, "I've got a mansion just over the hilltop, in that bright land where I'll never grow old. And someday yonder, I'll nevermore wander, but walk the streets there of purest gold."

What shape is your house in? When it's time to leave it empty, do you have a place reserved for your home to move into? If not, today's not a bit too soon to contact your spiritual Realtor. I'd be glad to refer you if you don't know Him already.

PARABLE OF THE FINISH LINE

Being the best friend of a dog has a way of teaching a variety of lessons. One can learn a lot about behavior, motivation, discipline, reward, loyalty...in short, about most of the major elements that define a satisfying relationship.

I've written about the days when I first took our English Setter, Cody, for the days' necessary walks. How he started each trek hauling on the lead as if he were the lead dog pulling a sled from Iditarod to Nome, Alaska. And of his last days when the only hauling he did was with a slight tug after we had completed our chores and it was time to return to the house.

However, with Suzy Q Mahoney, the mostly Black Lab to whom I belong, the behavior is slightly different. In this age of The Dog Whisperer, I've learned that I need to be the dominant one in our relationship...the one who sets the pace for these excursions...that I'm to be the one who determines when and where we go, when and where we stop. Wise female that she is, she allows me to continue in the impression that I'm the one in charge.

The other day, as we began our usual morning patrol, it was drizzling slightly...a condition about which Suzy is notably unenthusiastic. I had to continually tug on the lead and insist that she "Heel!" so that we could get the ritual leaving of offerings completed before we were soaked. She did not need encouragement, though, when we finally neared the house, where breakfast and her warm, dry corner were waiting.

That day was a contrast to more pleasant days when it's more appealing to be outdoors...when she must be coaxed by gentle, but insistent, tugs on the lead to return the last few feet of the way. On many of those days the prospect of going back inside holds little charm for Miss Suzy. For me, either, if the truth be told.

I've thought it's interesting to observe how people...and pets, as well...respond to the vision of the final laps of an endurance run, to the sight of that finish line in the distance. Some experience a burst of adrenalin-fueled energy that powers their exhausted bodies onward. Others feel a weariness and overwhelming sense of dread that they won't make it to the end.

We've seen videos of Olympic marathoners at the end of their endurance, as they enter the arena for the final lap, exhibit an apparent re-birth that buoys them up and propels them the final few meters to the finish. We've also seen some contestants so spent that they had to be coaxed and urged to take the remaining few steps to cross the finish line.

Although stock car racing isn't my favorite sporting event, I can't escape the excitement of watching the last few laps of some of the races...with the drivers striving urgently to extract the last few drops of power from their four-wheeled steeds, straining to be the first to be saluted by the fabled checkered flag. And then the final victory lap and the traditional burning of rubber as their spinning tires etch doughnuts into the track.

Recently, as I read a review of the Billy Graham book "Nearing Home," I thought about how each of us views life's race as we approach the unavoidable last laps and the eventual finish line. For the most part, I don't think we're very concerned about those things during the early and middle stage of the life event. It's only from the vantage point of age that we begin to take it seriously.

Each of us, as we progress thru life, has goals and expectations of things we intend to accomplish. For some, the race ends prematurely... before those goals have been achieved...before any thought has been directed toward preparing for the finish.

Unlike the marathon racer and the stock car driver, none of us knows the exact location of our individual finish line. We cannot tell how many more laps we have before we reach the final ones. Not many will know when it's time to put on that last burst of speed for the sprint to the winner's tape.

Here are some questions for you: Are you running the race as well as you can? Are you setting a pace that can serve as an inspiration, and guide for others yet to come? Is it time for you to pick up the pace? Are there failures for which you would like a "do-over"?

As you read this parable, I want to assure you that there's time for you to "run with patience the race that is set before you, looking unto Jesus." (Hebrews 12:1, 2) There's no need to regret and be hindered by those things you had hoped to accomplish but never quite got around to.

In the same verse, the writer to the Hebrews assured us that Jesus is the "author and finisher" of our faith. Did you get that? Not only is he the One Who wrote in our hearts the basis for our faith, but for those who put that faith in Him, He will see to it that all things will be properly finished.

Even though I don't know exactly where the finish line is I'm ready to start my sprint. How about you? Come on, let's make a dash for it!

PARABLE OF THE DISAPPOINTED DESIGNER

E very year I'm interested to note the fanfare and "hurrah" that are accorded to the awarding of the Nobel Prizes. According to Wikipedia, the will of Alfred Nobel specifies that this series of prizes is to be presented to "those who confer the 'greatest benefit on mankind' in physics, chemistry, peace, physiology or medicine, and literature."

If you are at all like I am, you may have wondered...even if only idly...about who this Nobel guy was, and what made him bequeath his millions in this manner. Was he just a do-gooder eccentric looking to make a name for himself? Like many in this internet age, I decided to answer that question by checking him out on Wikipedia, which is usually reliable as far as basic facts and history are concerned. Here's what I found:

"Alfred Nobel was born on 21 October 1833 in Stockholm, Sweden, into a family of engineers. He was a chemist, engineer, and inventor. In 1895 Nobel purchased the Boofers iron and steel mill, which he converted into a major armaments manufacturer. Nobel also invented ballistite, a precursor to many smokeless military explosives, especially cordite, the main British smokeless powder. Nobel amassed a fortune during his lifetime, most of it from his 355 inventions, of which dynamite is the most famous. In 1888, Alfred had the unpleasant surprise of reading his own obituary, titled 'The merchant of death is dead', in a French newspaper. As it was Alfred's brother Ludvig who had died, the obituary was eight years premature. Alfred was disappointed with what he read and concerned with how he would be remembered. This inspired him to change his will. On 10 December 1896 Alfred Nobel died in his villa in San Remo, Italy from a cerebral hemorrhage. He was 63 years old.

"To widespread surprise, Nobel's last will requested that his fortune be used to create a series of prizes for those who confer the 'greatest benefit on mankind' in physics, chemistry, peace, physiology or medicine, and literature. Nobel bequeathed 94% of his total assets, 31 million Swedish Krona (c. US $186 million in 2008), to establish the five Nobel Prizes. The executors of Nobel's will form the Nobel Foundation to take care of Nobel's fortune and organize the award of prizes."

So, this great prize...which has inspired and rewarded so many creative and productive thinkers in so many fields...resulted from the disappointment of a creative and productive designer as he contemplated what the world would think of him. Embarrassed that he might be remembered as "the merchant of death," he established the Foundation to correct his image.

I think about this story from time to time as I listen to reports in the media about events that take place daily. We read the news, see on television and hear on the radio, stories about people with various types of addictions...smoking, drugs, alcohol, gambling and, yes, now even sex...and the claim that the individuals are victims of illness that they are powerless to control, and for which they are not responsible. We are told that they were abused, have chemical imbalances, or faulty genes.

If you believe that God inspired the words that have become our Bible, there are certain truths that must be accepted as fact...

without apology or explanation. Yet, in spite of definite commands and statements on certain issues clearly defined in the Bible, mankind is determined to find fault with God's creation and His plans for His creatures, and find excuses for our errors.

Consider the Biblical prohibitions against sexual misbehavior, moral and ethical failings, and personal self-abuse. No matter that God dictated specific rules for each of these subjects...we hear daily about arguments claiming "that's not really what God meant. After all, He created us with these mental and physical disorders that we are helpless to resist. Surely, He won't hold them against us."

These human nature gurus would have us believe it's not the individual's fault if he or she is an adulterer, murderer, thief, liar or homosexual. They're convinced that it's because of social conditions... bad genes...situations that are not our fault...circumstances beyond our control.

They proclaim, "Don't blame us. Surely God can't hold us guilty of these acts when, after all, He made us this way." I'm sure God is constantly disappointed and embarrassed to discover how wrong He was to blame us and sentence us to eternal punishment when it's His fault.

Poor God. Think of all the apologies He'll have to make as He admits into the heavenly kingdom all these poor victims His Word condemned as "sinners."

Perhaps He should follow the example of Alfred Nobel and establish some sort of foundation to help define and correct His image before the world. Oh...that's right, He did. Isn't that the job of the Church? And didn't He award the original Peace Prize, available to all who follow His Son?

The prize awarded to each Believer isn't a medal, a certificate or a check, none of which will last. No, the Believer's Peace Prize actually *is* peace, and it will last throughout eternity. Have you won yours yet?

PARABLE OF THE DREAM CATCHER

Every once in a while, I recall an early *Beetle Bailey* cartoon— and if you're not a fan of the newspaper comics, he's the Army goldbrick created by Mort Walker. In this particular strip, Beetle awakens from an amazing dream and jumps from his bunk, searching for a pen and paper to write down the idea that he says will be "the answer to world peace."

As he goes from frame to frame in his search, the idea in a balloon over his head becomes dimmer and more jumbled. In the last frame Beetle sits with the much-sought pen and paper, but the balloon is empty...the world-saving idea has departed.

Sound familiar? It happens to me all the time...even this very morning.

Now, it is true that I have had maybe a half-dozen recurring dream themes during my life...the kinds of themes that a Dr. Freud might unravel to reveal some deep psychological meaning, perhaps. For the most part, however, my dreams seem to evaporate upon waking just as Beetle's did.

Specialists in the study of brain activity during sleep have determined that dreams are often the device used by the brain to deal with...and, often, to solve or settle...situations that we have confronted during the day. It isn't uncommon to hear of those who go to bed thinking about a problem and wake up with a possible solution in mind.

Many years ago, I read that one of the inventors of the modern sewing machine...there is a question whether it was Elias Howe or Isaac Singer...had a problem perfecting the mechanical action that would allow his machine to make a lockstitch. He recounted that after many hours and unsuccessful efforts he woke from a dream in which he was being attacked by a tribe of cannibals, each threatening him with a spear that had a hole in its point. A needle with the eye at the point was the solution he needed to make his invention of the lockstitch work properly...the result of a dream.

The other day I was standing at the kitchen sink, cleaning up after a meal, and something brushed my hair. I looked up and saw a familiar item that had been hung there several years ago by my wife. It was a souvenir brought home from a visit to one of the Native gift shops in Cherokee, North Carolina...a hand-crafted item called a Dream Catcher. Have you ever seen one?

These dream catchers can be found in all sizes and degrees of craftsmanship. They range from those small enough to be worn as earrings to large, elaborately finished wall hangings. Their basic design consists of a hoop shape with a more or less intricately woven web in the center and several feathers hanging down below. They are usually decorated with a variety of crystals and beads, colorful feathers and wrappings of rawhide or yarn.

Ours came with a small card that explained, "An old Indian legend says that the night air is filled with good and bad dreams. The dream catcher catches the dreams as they go by. The good dreams know the way and slip through the center hole, then slide gently down the soft feathers. The bad dreams, not knowing the way, get caught in the web and perish at first light. Dream catchers were hung on cradle boards and other places in the lodge for all to have good dreams."

There have been times when I would have liked to have a good dream catcher...either to channel good dreams into my brain, settle my thoughts and solve my problems, or to be an effective filter of those upsetting thoughts that sometimes trouble sleep.

The Bible tells us that God often used dreams to communicate His plans and instructions to those seeking to please Him and follow His will...to comfort and cheer fainting hearts. I'm satisfied from my own experience that He continues to do that today.

That's why, when I think of Dream Catchers, I picture the Hand of the Spirit directing some dreams into my subconscious and forbidding others from entering. That makes for sweet dreams.

PARABLE OF THE FINISHING TOUCH

One doesn't have to be especially aware of what's happening today to realize how much our daily lives are touched by sports. It's always been that way, I suppose, but with the combined influence of television, the internet and instant news reporting, the "Wide World of Sports" has, indeed, become the wide *world* of sports.

You can't get away from it. Think about it for a minute...it is almost impossible to pick up a newspaper or magazine, to tune in to a TV or radio program without coming across some reference to athletes, athletic events, or sporting equipment, or, for that matter, words and phrases that have been drawn from various athletic disciplines.

The earliest historians have offered accounts of the stress on athletic training as a technique for perfecting the skills necessary to wage...and win...wars. The first knowledge I had of this was in hearing reports of the original Olympic competitions. Why else would there have been events like running, wrestling, javelin and discus throwing, archery, chariot racing...? Mastery of these skills meant that one was likely to return safely from battle.

There was a time when each sport had a season. It's harder to find the line that divides one sport from another these days. Seems like baseball starts earlier and the World Series is later each year. Football, whether high school, college or professional begins in August and continues until the Super Bowl. When is that? February? March? July? With all the playoffs it's hard to tell. And basketball and soccer...well, forget about it. They never seem to end.

Whatever your idea of "sports" is, there is never a time when you can't find some current reference to it...or its practitioners...or its paraphernalia in the news or on-line somewhere. Even the Bible isn't a safe refuge from allusions to sports. The apostle Paul must himself have been an athlete, if his many mentions of fitness, fighting, striving and running races are any indication.

I have to admit, though, that there are many good and worthwhile lessons we can learn from the arena of sports. Two of them come to mind, and both were suggested by Bible studies. In a sense, they both have to do with follow-through, or the finishing touch.

To begin with, there can't be a good *follow*-through or a *finishing* touch without a good beginning. One has to show up prepared to complete the task...whatever it may be.

In John 13:3-5 we read about Jesus rising from the table and preparing to wash the feet of the disciples. Notice the details. He didn't simply pass the basin of water and the towel around so they could wash their own feet, the way a "leader" might do. He performed the act of washing in the manner of a servant, complete with the towel wrapped around His waist, and drying the feet carefully and completely Himself.

Our Savior got up prepared to do the complete job. And, in three years, completed His teaching about the Kingdom of God, and how to render God's loving blessings to those about us. Jesus began His task, and He continued...until He could say, "It is finished!"

Isn't the primary distinction between an amateur and a real pro to be seen in the follow-through? I'll always remember the experience of trying to coax one of our daughters to eat her first Brussels sprout. She stubbornly held it in her mouth for what seemed like hours until

I finally let her spit it out. To steal a line from one of the TV cooking shows, "There's no eating without swallowing." The finishing touch is what makes the difference.

However, as essential as the preparation is to successful completion, there comes a time to forget the past and DO something. The coach of a Youth League baseball team had spent days emphasizing the importance of keeping one's eye on the ball, to watch it all the way from the pitcher's hand to the bat. He was distressed during one game, though, to see a young batter keep his eye on the ball as it left the pitcher's hand, made contact with his bat and went soaring into the outfield...until he shouted, "Forget the ball and RUN!"

A good beginning requires follow-through. It depends upon moving from the preparation, into the action...and, finally, forgetting the past and concentrating on the present.

I once heard of a golf instructor who shared this bit of wisdom: "The power of the stroke is what moves the ball and determines distance. The follow-through determines its direction...where it will land." Whether the ball will hook, slice or fly straight down the fairway depends upon where the club is headed at the time of impact and where it winds up at the end of the stroke.

Just as in sports, it is true in all of life's activities. The success of our most sincere efforts depends as much on how we *finish* a task as it does on how the task was begun.

Jesus told the parable of the two sons who were asked by their father to perform a certain chore. The first said he would do it, but never followed through. The other son at first stubbornly refused, but had a change of heart and finished the job. In the final analysis, it was the finishing touch of the second son that drew the father's praise and approval.

There's an old maxim that says "Well begun is half done." However, many of us can confess to numbers of unfinished jobs that were well begun. I wonder if, perhaps, the reason that "the road to hell is paved with good intentions" is that the road to hell represents any route that finishes short of the destination that the Lord intended for us, His heavenly Kingdom.

A "good beginning" may indicate one's good intentions, but it represents nothing more than a start. To achieve the desired result, though, requires what my mom used to call "stick-to-it-ive-ness" ...perseverance, persistence, follow-through. It's the *finishing* touch that God blesses.

PARABLE OF THE COMPASS READING

I'll always remember my Uncle Hubert fondly, even though I only met him a few times when I was a boy. I recall him as very tall, with a broad grin when he was amused...and he talked funny, at least to the ear of a small Southern boy. After all, he had lived most of his adult life in Chicago.

My strongest memory of him was on the occasion when he came through Atlanta following his discharge from the Army after the end of World War II. Uncle Hubert stayed with us for several days, and in that short time became a hero to his young nephew.

Hubert had served in the Cavalry. I mean the *real* Cavalry...with horses! Imagine that. He gave me the spurs he had worn...even took an old belt and made new leather straps my size so I could wear them. And those weren't the only war treasures he left with me.

He gave me several souvenirs from his service in Europe...if I remember correctly, he fought in the Battle of the Bulge. He gave me several of his badges, including his Sharpshooter's pin.

But the real prizes were a number of items he took from German prisoners. The two things I recall most clearly are a pair of Nazi SS collar insignias and a soldier's field compass. Sadly, as is too often true of the stewardship of small boys, those wondrous treasures were enjoyed for a while and then disappeared into a black hole in time, lost forever. Sorry, Uncle Hubert.

However, that compass still exists in the mental safe of my memory, and I thought of it the other day, during the pastor's sermon on 2 Timothy 3:16. "All Scripture is given by inspiration of God, and is profitable for doctrine, for reproof, for correction, for instruction in righteousness, that the man of God may be complete, thoroughly equipped for every good work." (NKJV)

Let me explain why this verse brings the vision of Uncle Hubert's compass to mind. It tells us "All Scripture..."—not much, or even most...not portions carefully selected to prove a point...but *all*—originates with God, and is breathed out upon us by Him.

"...is profitable for doctrine..." Scripture faithfully teaches doctrine. Doctrine is a principle, or body of principles taught as truth relating to a system of belief. No matter what map one chooses to use with it, that compass will unfailingly point to the true magnetic north. It is reliable.

"...for reproof..." When we stray from the principles expressed in Scripture, its guidelines give us a clear indication of our error. When properly oriented with a map, the compass can accurately show how far we have gone off course...and in which direction.

"...for correction..." Knowledge of sin isn't enough. Scriptures tell us not only that we have failed to obey God's principles, but what we must do to be returned to His path. As the Roman jailer asked, "What must I do to be saved?" Scripture shows us. My German compass had a viewfinder which would allow one to set a course, using topographic features, and make way in that direction. There was also a scale along one edge for use in measuring distance on a map. Those two things also made it easier to estimate how to get back on track after going off course.

"...for instruction in righteousness..." Teaching of doctrine is the necessary foundation for establishing faith. Scripture not only provides that foundation, but it provides needed guidelines for continuing development and growth in faith. The faithful compass, when checked regularly and carefully, will allow its user to keep on the path straight toward the goal.

There is a type of sporting event called orienteering, where the participants compete in time trials, finding their way from the starting point to an unknown destination over strange terrain, using only their compass and a map. Living the Christian life is a lot like spiritual orienteering, isn't it?

Working your way through life's territory is a lot more peaceful and satisfying when you rely on the Word of God as your map and compass. Have you checked your compass readings today?

PARABLE OF THE
MAÑANA PRINCIPLE

When I was a boy—much longer ago than I want to think about right now—there was a song made popular by Bing Crosby and the Andrews Sisters (I told you it was a long time ago) that finished each verse with the chorus "Mañana, mañana, mañana is good enough for me." I'm afraid that there have been far too many days in my life when that could have been my theme song.

We've all heard the story about the man whose wife complained about the leaky roof and nagged him about fixing it. His response was, "Well, when it's raining, I can't fix it...when it's not raining it don't leak." One excuse is as good as another when you don't want to do something.

For too many years I have lived in peaceful coexistence with many of those things that need to be done...waiting for the Spirit to move me to take care of them. My wife Lyn understood that tendency all too well, and so was ready to hold me accountable...at least for the most urgent items on either her list or mine.

Don't get me wrong. I don't think I'm quite as bad as the fellow who bragged, "I'm not a bit afraid of hard work. I can lie down right beside it and sleep like a baby." But I do have my issues.

When my Internal Monitor registers something that needs to be done, my Mental Effort Allocator measures the degree of urgency, weighs the relative importance of the project, coordinates that with the list of other items already analyzed...then adds it to the list to be tackled "mañana"...tomorrow. Or at least postponed until someone steps up to hold me accountable.

This matter of accountability is one of the natural problems with being in business for oneself...as I have been for most of my working career. In a typical job there are always those above and below one in the organization chart, whose own progress depends upon how one handles those tasks that are set before him or her.

That responsibility isn't nearly so clearly defined when one sets one's own agenda. It's much too easy to mute the volume on that Internal Monitor, and engage one's Mental Effort Allocator when one simply doesn't want to do something, isn't it?

If I'm not careful, I can walk right past something that is out of place, listen to my IM intone, "That's not where that belongs!" and hear my MEA respond, "I'll have to put that away soon." And, since I was on my way to handle something more or less urgent, the misplaced object remains misplaced until I begin the search for it next time it's needed.

Every time I call myself into account for yielding to the mañana principle I promise myself to do better. After all, I have done better at times, keeping things in their proper place...putting them back in that proper place as soon as I was finished using them...being able to put my hand on them the next time they were needed. Then, after congratulating myself at being so well organized, I suffer a relapse and have to start all over again...mañana.

My Dad said to me...more than once..."Son, if you can *think* about it today, you can *work* on it today. Don't put it off 'til tomorrow." He also often said, "Do *something*...even if it's wrong! You can correct something that was done wrong, but not something you haven't done."

There was a time when every office in the IBM organization had a wall plaque that read, "THINK." Under later management philosophy those signs were altered to read, "Don't THINK...WORK!" Dad was ahead of IBM with that ethic.

229

The Bible tells us not to be concerned about tomorrow...that there is plenty that needs to be, and can be, done today. None of us can count upon a mañana when all those things will be done.

Of all the items that exist on my Mañana List, there is one that I'm more convicted about than any of the others. I've grouped quite a few activities under the heading "Be Jesus to someone today." I've just realized as I write this paragraph that there are several names I need to move from "Mañana" to "Ahora"...Now. I'll bet a look at your list will reveal the same thing. Am I right?

PARABLE OF THE JCC SYNDROME

I've driven past it many times over the years...at least twice a week, sometimes more...but on this occasion, after the time change from Daylight Savings to Standard Time, darkness had come and the sign was lighted. At least part of it was.

The sign which proudly promised "Complete Auto Care" in the daylight, now simply challenged "Care." The rest of the sign was dark. It's not a big sign...the road on which the company is located, though fairly busy, isn't the most traveled in the area by far. Most of the drivers passing by probably didn't even notice its quiet urging. Care.

I felt like a character in one of those quirky, surreal movies...the one person in the whole world who registers the clues evident in his surroundings and follows them to the solution to whatever problem is threatening his universe. Care.

As a reader of these Parables, you may already have guessed that this one-word imperative served as a mental speed-bump which focused my attention and changed the direction of my thoughts. Care. What an interesting suggestion.

For the better part of two generations technological developments have made it possible as never before for one to conduct one's activities... whether for business, personal or social reasons...without the necessity to actually communicate face to face with another person. Almost instantly we can be in touch with almost anyone, almost anywhere in the world...without a care...almost.

Relationships that formerly took time to establish and develop... time which allowed us to learn about each other and allowed friendships to grow naturally...now can spring up in this digital, on-line age like hot-house plants, artificially propagated, quickly grown, and ultimately short-lived.

With e-mail, iPhones and Bluetooth...Google, Bing and Yahoo...Facebook, Twitter and the Lord only knows what other social substitute...it's now perfectly acceptable, even expected, to "Friend," "Like," "Accept," "Ignore," and even "Delete" someone without ever knowing them...or caring about them. Care.

The most recent time I passed the Care sign, I came to my computer and looked up one of my favorite folk duos, the Smothers Brothers. I can't say that I necessarily agree with all of their political views, but they made some valid points with their humor and they are still truly funny and talented. The sign reminded me of one of their comedy routines that I simply had to revisit.

The routine which came to mind was their rendition of the old folk song "Jimmy Crack Corn." That's it playing right this minute in one of your mind's back rooms. They begin the song normally, "Jimmy crack corn and I don't care, Jimmy crack corn and I don't care..." then Tommy begins to repeat over and over, "I don't care, I don't care..." Dick stops singing and says, "That's not the way the song goes!" To which Tommy retorts, "I don't care!" Funny stuff...at least to me.

The problem I see with the age in which we live is that it has become all too easy for one to look around at the spectacular and often troubling events occurring in the world and demonstrate the JCC (Jimmy Crack Corn) Syndrome..."I don't care!" It's simpler to hit the Disallow or the Delete button in the back of the brain and forget about those unpleasant and disagreeable items.

So, you see why that Care sign with its quiet but insistent urging struck a responsive chord. Much like those more strident hippy protest signs of the sixties and early seventies that read "Give A Damn!" If only everyone could...and would...Give A Damn. And Care.

Got too many cares and worries of your own to think about those around you? Perhaps you should trust Jesus and follow the advice of Scripture, "casting all your cares upon Him, for He cares for you." Then, you can put away the JCC Syndrome for good, follow the sign...and Care.

PARABLE OF THE FULL-SERVICE PROMISE

You hear them all the time...probably have said them yourself many times...when friends, family and even mere acquaintances part: "Come back to see us soon" ...or "Call me" ...or "I'll be praying for you." And the automatic, polite responses are usually "I will," "I will," and "I'll be praying for you, too."

Let's face it...for the most part, no one expects those invitations or those responses to be taken seriously. They are simply part of a system of etiquette recognized by civilized people everywhere...a matter of custom.

When you meet someone on the street and greet them with "How are you today?", most people understand that isn't an inquiry into their state of health. A lengthy lecture on the person's current trials and tribulations isn't expected or called for.

And how many times, upon hearing of the difficulties and challenges facing the person to whom you're speaking, have you offered, "If there's anything I can do, please don't hesitate to call me"? Just another courteous cliche most of us fall back on when we can't think of anything helpful to say.

I like the advice one writer gave. "Don't tell someone to call 'if there is anything' you can do to help. Think of something helpful to do...and *do* it. That's true friendship and meaningful help."

When I graduate to the Kingdom and the Divine Appraiser takes a look at the page of my Life's accomplishments, I'll not be surprised to see the disappointment in His eyes as He looks down the list of offers of help and promises to pray for individuals in genuine need of them...only to look across the ledger to see how quickly those promises were forgotten...those offers not acted upon. I don't think of myself as mean, or hypocritical, or uncaring. But I'm afraid that I do make these polite promises without following through on them. How about you?

Recently, as I was selecting hymns for an Order of Service at my church, I chose one of my favorites, "How Firm a Foundation." One of the reasons I like it so much is that the second verse is taken from Isaiah 41:10, where Jehovah tells Israel through His prophet, "Fear not, for I am with thee: be not dismayed; for I am thy God; I will strengthen thee; yea, I will help thee; yea, I will uphold thee with the right hand of my righteousness."

As a Sunday School teacher, I looked at this passage closely over the years and found that it is much deeper than it appears. It's not one of our "Y'all come" statements. It is a true, Full-Service Promise. Let me explain what I mean.

The Lord begins with a statement that any of us could make, and it isn't subject to any form of proof or analysis: "Don't be afraid. I'm here with you. No need to be upset." Easy to say, right? That's the sort of thing any good friend or caring acquaintance might tell us when we're in trouble.

Here's where the Full-Service begins to be meaningful. Notice how often the personal ID of God is used: "I am." And the logical extension of that ID: "I will." The Lord is saying, "Because I am Who I say I am, you can count upon My promises." Now it really gets impressive.

The hymn verse adds, "I will still give thee aid," as a prelude to the promise, "I will strengthen Thee..." God designed us with Free

Will, to stand on our own two feet and face the trials and challenges of life. But He knew there would be times our resistance would be low, our resources diminished. Those are the times He promises to give us additional physical and spiritual strength.

Next, He promises, "Yea, I will help thee..." Our God isn't content to merely give us an energy boost and leave us to struggle on our own. He promises to step in and fight by our side, covering our backs, so to speak.

However, even that assistance is not always enough to carry us through the daily battles. There are those times when we become so weary, so badly wounded in our spirits that we can no longer stand our ground. He promises that in those times when collapse and failure are about to overcome us, He will literally step in, put His arms around us and support us in our weakness with the strength of His righteousness. "Yea, I will uphold thee with the right hand of my righteousness."

I hope that the next time I'm tempted to give one of those proper, polite responses to one who has genuine need, that I'll be able to remember the Full-Service Promise of our God...and be prepared to be that kind of friend who encourages, abides with, and renders meaningful help as a testimony to the Lord Who has never failed me. Will you join me? Promise?

PARABLE OF THE LIFE AUDITION

I've been singing in one type of group or another since I was in Miss Bell's fifth grade at Park Street School in Marietta. That was the year they announced that there were openings in the Marietta Boy Choir for any that wanted to join.

It seemed that the only problem was that boys had to walk from their schools all over Marietta to the Episcopal church in downtown Marietta twice a week for choir practice. In order to get there in time we would have to leave school thirty minutes early on those days. That was *so* not a problem for me. I suspect Miss Bell was glad to be relieved of me for a while as well.

The only requirement for this indulgence was our faithful attendance at all rehearsals. Mrs. Ogden needed bodies...and if they were attached to voices that could make a pleasing sound, so much the better. I was placed in the alto section. I didn't know what that meant exactly, except that I never got to sing melody. Bummer.

In high school I played some football, was a member of the Rifle Team and the Drama Club and was in the College Prep curriculum, so I didn't have a lot of time to think about singing. In Spring of my Junior year, the announcement came over the PA system that the sign-up list for the Spring Talent Show was on the bulletin board outside the office for anyone who was interested. I was interested...I signed up...I was in.

In my Senior year I had room for an elective subject, and since my "steady," Judy, was in the Choir, I decided to sign up for that. Mr. Lowrance, the director, needed some basses for the Special Choir, and I was singing Bass at that time. I was in.

While I was at Georgia Tech, and later as a young married person, I sang in several community opera groups in the Atlanta area. They were always looking for male voices, so all one had to do was show up ready to sing. I showed up...I was in. I've often joked that one could always find me listed in the program under my stage name: "And Chorus."

In many years of showing up and being accepted simply because they needed somebody...anybody...there were also plenty of events and groups that I wanted to join, parts I wanted to sing, roles I wanted to play. I went to a number of auditions without being chosen.

It has occurred to me that so many of the activities in which I have been able to participate, and which have been such a source of enjoyment and pleasure, have taken me in like the great maw of a sperm whale takes in whatever krill happens to be in its path. No selection...no discriminating choice...just a matter of "right place, right time."

I've wondered many times why it is that so many of the things I have set my hopes on and tried out for have not worked out for me, while the things that I get into almost by accident seem to be so much better suited to my talents and abilities. Is it coincidence? I don't believe it.

As I look back upon all these experiences, here's what I have learned: We all go through life much like the way a small child goes through a cafeteria line. We see this, and that, and the other attractive food and want it all...especially the dessert. As my mom used to tell us, "Your eyes are bigger than your stomach." And we often want things that may not be good for us.

During my lifetime I've "auditioned" for many things for which I wasn't suited, that would have been harmful for me. I have gone after things simply because I wanted them...suitable or not.

My Lord loves me and hasn't stopped me from wanting and going after those things. But, in His wisdom and foreknowledge, He has led me into the path of those things that He knew were good and right for me...things for which He had equipped me...and allowed me to select them. Isn't that the only type of Life Audition that counts?

PARABLE OF THE GOOD DAYS

"I'm not sure I like this new style of worship."

"Well, I'm sure...I don't like it a bit. I got so much more out of the old services."

"Me, too. Now there is so much noise and racket that I go home with a headache."

"I hate to sound negative, but so do I. I know there are some of the young people that actually enjoy this kind of thing...bless their hearts. All I know is that I feel like I'm being pummeled all over every time they light into those drums."

"And everybody flailing away on those strings, and singing so fast and loud I can hardly hear myself think. God only knows what they're saying. And those trumpets...well, don't get me started."

"And did you notice that some of them were so excited they were almost dancing...right there in front of God and everybody?"

"Frankly, it's all so distracting that I find it hard to worship. It's true that the Tabernacle is lovely, but I just don't understand why Moses didn't leave things the way they used to be. Sometimes I think that Egypt wasn't all that bad after all."

I'll bet I know what you're thinking. Unless you are among those few who have a broader vision than most, you were beginning to find your place on one side or the other of the generation fence. I firmly believe that there hasn't been a single generation since Eden that hasn't expressed a desire for the young folks to leave well enough alone...stick with the tried-and-true methods...stop trying to change the world.

When Og...or was it his uncle? chiseled the rough edges off that large stone to make what he called a "wheel," his parents probably said, "That lazy lout will never amount to anything. All he ever thinks about is how to get out of good, hard work."

Can you imagine the early scribes complaining, "First they did away with clay tablets. Those things would last forever. Those lambskin parchments were bad enough to work with and file. Now they expect us to keep our permanent records on *papyrus*. That's nothing but ground up stems and leaves, you know. Sure...like that'll work."

Or, how about, "Scholarship is a thing of the past since they started teaching common rabble to read and write. Now anyone who can hold a quill thinks his writing is worth reading. And, I heard the other day that some idiot has invented something called a pencil, where you don't even have to stop and think what to write next while you dip your pen in ink. Not only that, but they have even started putting a rubber ball on the end of it, so that no matter how many mistakes you make you can rub them out and start all over. No...this is the end of careful, well-thought-out composition."

When I was at Georgia Tech a computer was a thing of substance, an electronic marvel, capable of hundreds of thousands of calculations in seconds. The hardware could occupy an entire building...the software, even more. Today's Information Technologists have been spoiled by the development of computers that can fit into a coat pocket, capable of all that those monster machines could do, as fast as one can manipulate their keyboards.

I once heard some engineering professors discussing the sorry state of education when the school began to allow students to rely on those new pocket calculators for their computations instead of the trusty slide rule that each incoming freshman had to purchase and master. "How are they going to learn to estimate?" argued one educator. How, indeed...or why?

I began this piece with a reference to changing attitudes about worship. With something as personal, and at the same time as widespread, as worship, it should come as no surprise that there have always been disagreements between at least two groups of faithful and dedicated believers.

There are those who want to make worship more attractive to those who have no background in its purpose and practice, and those who think that the church should stick with the techniques and practices that have been proven to change lives over long spans of time. In my opinion, no single approach should be thought of as the only...or even as the best...form of worship for believers.

I believe I have written before about the introduction to the 1975 edition of the Baptist Hymnal, where the compilers wrote: "Congregational singing has not always been a common practice in Baptist churches. Some churches in both England and America in the seventeenth century offered vigorous opposition to 'promiscuous singing' (the singing of believers and unbelievers together) and the singing of 'set forms' (the metrical versions of the psalms because they were 'man made'). However, congregational singing prevailed and continues to be a vital force in Christian worship and fellowship among Baptists."

So... here's where the Lord has led me on the subject of things old and new: Simply because a thing is old doesn't necessarily mean that it is good; nor does it follow that something good must necessarily be old. Whether we're talking about forms of worship or social customs... whether we prefer experimenting with the new and innovative or relying in the familiar and proven...don't dispose of the old *because* it is old, and don't embrace the new *because* of its newness.

One of my favorite quotations to lift out of its Biblical context is from Jesus' admonition that "this ought you to have done and not left the other undone." No matter how good past days may have been, there'll be plenty of good days to come, too. Don't miss out on the possible joy of tasting the new because you're clutching too tightly that which is old.

PARABLE OF THE PETTY STUFF

I have a confession to make. I make it freely and without duress. For many years I have been a closet fan of the late comedian George Carlin. A closet fan because he could be rude, crude and vulgar at times...at times I was embarrassed for anyone to know that he made me laugh.

One of Carlin's lines that came to mind this morning was, "Don't sweat the petty stuff...and don't pet the sweaty stuff." As another of my favorite comedians, Larry the Cable Guy, would say, "Now that's funny, I don't care who you are." I don't know...maybe it's just me.

That quote popped into my head like one of those pop-up notes on my computer, as I gently massaged a sore ankle while trying to come up with a subject for today's writing. The ankle was sore because I had trespassed upon the campground of a gypsy band of yellow jackets that had taken possession of a small part of my back yard. One of the band's brave sentinels attacked me and my lawnmower, and during our hasty retreat inflicted a wound on my ankle. (Now, wasn't that a lot more colorful than saying, "I got stung while trying to mow over a yellow jackets' nest"?)

I don't know that I am particularly allergic to insect bites and stings, but I do know that I seem to suffer large welts from even the smallest gnat-bite, so I wasn't surprised to experience some swelling and painful itching around the location of the sting. "Big deal," I told myself, "You got a bee sting. Get over it." That was three days ago.

Have you ever stopped to think how much of one's life is affected by such petty stuff? It could be a tiny splinter in a finger...a hammer-mashed thumb...a skinned elbow...even a yellow jacket sting on the ankle. The total surface area of the afflicted part may be insignificant, but the ability of that petty incident to affect our happiness and comfort can be tremendous.

During much of the day there are multiple distractions to keep our minds occupied. There are sounds, smells and sights competing for the next available synapses (the passing of impulses from nerve cell to nerve cell) like patrons waiting for the next free table at a popular restaurant.

However, when those peaks pass...when the sensual rush hour is over...there's always a chance that the petty stuff will begin to nag for our attention. That's why those toothaches or coughs...or yellow jacket stings...always seem to be at their worst at bedtime.

There are several things to be learned from our observation of the petty stuff in life. First, it's important to understand that no part of our body can be effective without the rest of the body. Therefore, no problem is so petty or insignificant that it is not felt throughout the whole body. When one-part hurts, everything hurts. When my ankle was attacked, the whole body went into action to get away from danger. There's no need to surrender to the petty stuff. Use all your resources to fight.

Second, there are times when we can expect to be more sensitive to the discomfort inflicted by petty things. It's good to be prepared for those episodes and not be distressed by them...to keep in mind that they will pass.

Finally, the Lord knows the toll that the petty stuff can take on our store of joy...and He knows that the adversary will try to take advantage of any weakness on our part. Jesus promised He would never leave us or forsake us...and He didn't mean only when we're faced with the huge, important issues of life. He is also with us to face the petty stuff...and let's face it, in His eyes, it's *all* petty stuff.

PARABLE OF THE WEEPING CHERRY'S PROMISE

I had to call a special meeting in my mental conference room to brainstorm some ideas for this Parable. Self, Ego, Id, Superego...we were all present. As usual with such meetings, there was a lot of argument and banging on the mental table for emphasis.

At issue was what the title should be. This was to be a follow-up and development of the Parable of The Weeping Cherry, which appeared in "*More Parables*". Part of me wanted to copy the movie industry with a name like "Parable of The Return of the Weeping Cherry," or "Parable of The Weeping Cherry II."

My twelve-year-old self liked the Saturday Western sound of "Son of the Parable of The Weeping Cherry," or "Parable of The Weeping Cherry Rides Again." My marketing alter-ego, Ad Man, finally won out, though, with the title, "Parable of The Weeping Cherry's Promise."

This spirited skull-session lasted all the way to church on that morning. It was peacefully concluded and all parties were satisfied by the time I pulled into the parking lot. I was relieved, because not all my internal battles are resolved that easily or quickly.

In case you haven't read the Parable of The Weeping Cherry, or have forgotten what it's about, I'll give you a little summary. Back in the bleak days of Fall I described the appearance of a Weeping Cherry tree that I passed frequently. It had shut down for the season and could easily pass for dead. I pointed out that, like many of our experiences in life, no matter how bad things seem to be, there is always reason to have hope for a new burst of life.

Well...sure enough, on the Spring morning when I passed that once lifeless-looking tree, I could see clear signs of that promised, much-anticipated rebirth. Delicate, pink blossoms once more were cautiously spreading along the graceful arcs of the Cherry's umbrella-like branches. Minute green leaves were tentatively working their way into the company of those blossoms as if testing the atmosphere before resuming the responsibility for bargaining with the sun for the resources to keep the tree alive and growing.

Of course, all the plants, shrubs and trees are showing that same evidence of rebirth; the resurgence of life clearly visible in the first self-conscious blossoms and leaf buds as at first, they creep out like bashful children. Then, reassured by the warmth of the Spring sun and encouraged by the abundant rain of the season, they burst out with the joyous abandon of their youth.

Oh, I knew in the Fall that this would happen. It happens every year. In fact, one of the first Scripture verses, I learned as a child in Vacation Bible School was Genesis 8:22, where God promised Noah, "While the earth remained, seedtime and harvest, and cold and heat, and summer and winter, and day and night shall not cease." That was the firm promise of the Lord, himself—in spite of the stern and frightening predictions of today's global warming or climate change enthusiasts.

The American Film Institute has published a list of the top 100 most famous quotations from the movies that would make for a very entertaining trivia quiz. Number thirty-seven on the list is, "I'll be back!" In case you don't remember that one, it's the reassuring promise made by the Terminator, played by Arnold Schwarzenegger, whose real-life role was as governor of California.

As reassuring as that promise was to the young star of the movie, it can't come close to the power of Jesus's promise when He predicted that, although He would die on the cross, He would rise again, and come back. And He did as He promised.

In my mind, that is the promise illustrated by the rebirth of the Weeping Cherry. No matter how bleak and hopeless one may feel, for all who have been reborn in Christ, the hope of a new beginning—a resurrection—is valid and reliable. After all, He promised.

PARABLE OF THE POOR EXCUSE

Every once in a while, something really clever will be circulated on the internet, whether in forwarded e-mails or one of the so-called social media, like Facebook or Twitter. I received one the other day...a picture taken to look like a police mug shot. The subject was a sullen and bedraggled calico cat glaring unrepentantly into the camera. The caption read, "The dog started it."

I rank that alongside the daily comic strip "The Family Circus," where the children have two imaginary friends named "Ida Know" and "Not Me." As you would expect, these two characters were the accused perpetrators of all the mischief and mayhem that occurred in the home.

It hasn't been all that long ago that the comedian Flip Wilson created a character he called Geraldine, who was always getting into some kind of trouble. Her excuse was always, "The devil made me do it."

One of the unavoidable characteristics of human nature is our tendency to explain and excuse our way out of the unfavorable consequences of our decisions and actions. "It's not our fault," the social commentators might say, "we've been this way since Adam and Eve were in the Garden of Eden." Another excuse.

True enough, when confronted by the Lord after sampling the forbidden fruit, Adam said, "The woman...who, by the way, *you* created...that woman gave me the fruit. She's the one who picked it, and she tasted it first."

Eve wasn't going to stand there and take the rap alone, either. She excused herself with, "Well, I wouldn't have thought about trying that fruit if that serpent over there hadn't talked me into it. I'll never know why you let that creepy creature into the garden anyway."

In all fairness, the serpent is the only one who didn't try to blame someone else. I imagine him just lying there...or standing, or sitting, or coiled, for that matter...licking the air and smirking at the thought of what suckers we humans are. How easily we are deceived. He was... and still is...happy to be our poor excuse for our failures.

In the recent *Parable of The Deferred Payment*, I referred to Exodus 32 and the incident of the Golden Calf. You remember the story. Moses had been on the Mount with God, receiving the Ten Commandments, for forty days and nights. The Israelites quickly forgot the providence of God in bringing them through the Red Sea and providing for them in the Wilderness.

The people prevailed upon Aaron to make them an idol to represent the God they couldn't see and whose representative was no longer in the camp. Aaron collected their golden jewelry and fashioned it into a calf, which they proceeded to worship with singing and wild revelry.

When Moses confronted Aaron—after grinding the idol into powder and making the people drink it—Aaron whined, "Don't blame me. You were gone so long the people made me make an idol to lead them, so I took their gold jewelry and threw it into the fire and Lo! and behold! that calf just came out by itself."

There's more to the story, but that's enough to make my point. The Bible is filled with stories of people offering excuses for bad behavior...as well as for their failure to act at all. Even Jesus observed in one of His parables, "and they began with one accord to make excuse."

Whether poor excuses or perfectly legitimate ones, they are all intended to justify our decisions and explain our actions...to make us look better to observers and critics, and to absolve us of blame for any unfavorable outcomes.

The Bible is clear on this subject, however. It cautions us that "we are without excuse," and "there is none righteous, no not one." A well-crafted excuse will serve us no better than a poor one when we come to that time of trial and judgment promised to each and all. None will escape the penalty to be exacted when those excuses are rejected.

None...except for those who have given up making excuses and pled guilty...surrendered themselves to the only One Who could pre-pay the penalty for their misdeeds and wrongdoing. That One, of course, is Jesus and He is ready to relieve you of the burden of all those poor excuses...to write one final and complete excuse that will always be true and that will never expire.

PARABLE OF THE SMILE SOLUTION

S mile though your heart is aching
  Smile even though it's breaking.
  When there are clouds in the sky you'll get by.
If you smile through your pain and sorrow
Smile and maybe tomorrow
You'll see the sun come shining through
For you.

Light up your face with gladness,
Hide every trace of sadness.
Although a tear may be ever so near
That's the time you must keep on trying
Smile, what's the use of crying.
You'll find that life is still worthwhile-
If you just smile.

- Charlie Chaplin

That song has been reverberating through the halls of my memory for several days now...most often buoyed along on the voice of Nat "King" Cole. It all started with an episode of The Doctors TV show. The topic of one of their segments was the therapeutic value of smiling.

The Doctors didn't cite any scientific test results...other than the anecdotal evidence of the "experts tell us" variety...but I think most of us will agree with their conclusions. Among other things, they said that smiling decreases stress, relieves tension, improves one's mood as well as the moods of those nearby. Not only does smiling seem to improve one's general health, but it can also make the day of others more pleasant.

The Creed of Optimists International includes the admonition, "Promise yourself...to give every living creature you meet a smile." Broadway performers offer the advice, "Gray skies are going to clear up. Put on a happy face." Even popular singers observe "When you're smiling, when you're smiling, The whole world smiles with you."

I once had a poster showing Snoopy, from the Peanuts cartoon, doing his happy dance over the caption "Smile at everyone you meet today. It'll make them wonder what you've been up to."

I recall seeing one of the classic silent movies on a late-night TV special. One of the famous Gish sisters portrayed a girl who had been beaten by her drunk boxer father. Before the camera faded out, it showed a close-up of her face as she used her fingers to turn up the corners of her mouth into a wan smile, in a mute promise to the audience that she would be all right.

I've thought a lot over the years about the powerful effects of the simple smile. I've observed that even the grumpiest and morose faces of strangers on the street can be converted into some semblance of a smile...albeit grudgingly...when you look them in the eye and give them a big grin.

What is it about a sincere smile that can soothe a sobbing child, soften the bitterest debate, shed sunlight on the gloomiest day, offer

encouragement, boost confidence and restore flagging courage? And it's not just a trick you can use on others. Try smiling at yourself in the mirror.

Someone (Was it me? I can't be sure.) once said that a smile is the lens through which God shines His light to brighten the way of a weary and worried world. Try it and see if it works for you.

PARABLE OF THE PIGEONHOLE PRINCIPLE

S ince I committed myself to writing these parables on a regular basis, I've accumulated quite a few. As each one is completed, I save it to a folder within a file labeled "Parables." Every time I want to re-read one...or refer to it for some reason...or send it to someone...I fire up the old computer and wend my way through the root path, following the digital breadcrumbs to the particular piece for which I'm looking. Isn't that a neat and organized way to keep track of things?

As marvelous as the computer is, it has nothing to compare with the human brain. I've been told that the human brain automatically records everything the body's senses experience at every moment of time...and stores that information throughout a lifetime. In fact, it has been theorized that every human has what we have come to call, in our moments of wonder, a photographic memory.

You might rightly question, "If I have such a memory, with its 'Record' button permanently pressed, why is it I have such a hard time recalling pertinent bits of information whenever I need them?" Here's the interesting part. Although we each have perfect memory banks, recording and retaining all of life's bits of data, not all of us have effective filing and retrieval systems.

For most of us...dare I say 'normal' people?...a trip through our brains' data banks would be like one of those visits the TV show takes through the home of a compulsive hoarder...edging sideways through piles and stacks of accumulated "stuff."

So...the trick to remembering the things we want to retain is simply to learn a system of data organization to make it possible to retrieve the information we need at a specific time. Developing and perfecting that system is what we call Education.

The basic foundation for learning is understanding how to use the same principles we apply when we operate a computer...setting up Files, Folders and Sub-Folders so that each bit of information can be quickly and accurately traced and retrieved. Simple, huh?

As with any system, however, this technique is not without its dangers and problems. There are times when an item of information doesn't fit neatly into any of the established Files, Folders and Sub-Folders. What must we do then?

Typically, we'll simply shoehorn it into whatever seems to be the nearest and most logical pigeonhole and, maybe, mark it with a mental asterisk to remind us that it's a special case. And, as a special case, it may or may not be distinguished from other items in that compartment.

There are a couple of definitions of the word "pigeonhole" that I find interesting. "To classify mentally; categorize." And, "To put aside and ignore; shelve."

(I saw that yawn. I'll get to my point.)

Not only do we put bits of data into these pigeonholes, but we tend to do the same thing with people...both as individuals and as groups. And once they have been conveniently filed, we feel entirely justified in assuming that each person in the group has the same characteristics as all others we have placed there.

Keep that in mind each time you hear someone refer to a class, group or category of people by a label...whether Blonde or Redhead,

Northerner or Southerner, Conservative or Liberal, Democrat or Republican. And be especially suspicious any time someone uses one of those labels preceded by the modifier "All."

Throughout history some of the greatest injustices have been perpetrated upon groups and classes of people simply because of the pigeonhole into which they had been sorted. Whether by race, nation, economic or social status, religion, philosophy or level of education... the pigeonhole principle has been the basis for more prejudice, discrimination and mistreatment than any other judgment system.

Very few of us are called upon to deal with large groups of people...with everyone in a particular pigeonhole. Why not give each individual his own pigeonhole and treat him with consideration of those traits and characteristics that make him unique? It's not likely that you will be in a position to influence everyone in a larger pigeonhole anyway.

Keep in mind that the Bible states clearly that the Creator of the entire Universe will sit in final judgment, not over categories of people in pigeonholes...grouped for His convenience...but dealing with the life of each individual in one specific detail. Each of us will be measured, not based upon the value of a group classification, but by one fact alone.

The determining factor in our final Judgment will be whether or not we accepted the price paid to cover the penalty for our failure to please God. To paraphrase the Scripture, "There is no other label, or pigeonhole, by which ye must be saved."

If you have accepted those terms for your forgiveness, I suggest that each time you pause today to put anything in its pigeonhole where it belongs, you stop and thank the Lord for labeling you as one of His "pigeons."

PARABLE OF THE SALT SHAKER

I have a confession to make. For a large part of my life, I was the victim of a habit that dismayed some, disgusted others and, if they had known about it, would have caused certain psychologists to nod knowingly and make notes on their memo pads.

I was a compulsive and enthusiastic food salter...no need to taste it first, I just gestured with the shaker vigorously over everything, like a native shaman warding off evil spells. Maybe that's a good analogy... since I never experienced any food poisoning after following that ritual.

I'm sure that good cooks and fine chefs everywhere shook their heads in disapproval any time I attacked their carefully prepared delights in such a disrespectful manner, but I was totally under the control of my addiction. No matter that it spoiled the subtle flavors of delicately seasoned entrees. No matter that it has since been found to be unhealthy. No matter.

It is also true that I haven't completely overcome my saline dependency. I still apply liberal doses of salt to three things: corn on the cob, sliced tomatoes, and food I'm not particularly fond of. The first two because I love the flavor...the others because I don't.

In fairness to myself, however, I should point out that my habits have changed over the course of the last third of my life, and I seldom salt anything, except for the three I've mentioned, without first tasting it. Even then salting isn't the compulsion it used to be.

I thought about my former saline problem the other night as I was preparing a meal, following the instructions as any good neophyte chef should. "Simmer for 25 to 30 minutes and season to taste," I was directed. Then I did what I never would have done before. I actually tasted it to see how much salt, etc., it needed. I was so proud of myself.

There is one slight disadvantage to this decrease in salt dependency, though...it's not serious, but it can be annoying at times. In the humidity of the kitchen, salt in the shaker tends to settle in, clump up, plug the holes and resist efforts to apply it to the place where it's needed. That's why, when I tried to "season to taste," I couldn't get it to pour.

While I attempted to correct that situation, there were several grains of thought that kept rattling around in my mental salt cellar.

First, no matter how well designed and artfully decorated the salt shaker may be, it is nothing more than an attractive table decoration while the salt remains inside. Salt in the shaker is useless. It is only when the salt leaves the shaker that it can fulfill its intended purpose. Only then can it lend its flavor wherever it's applied.

Second, salt must be applied thoughtfully. We all know how quickly the finest meal can be ruined by pouring on too much or too little salt. The salt will also be more effective when it is applied at the proper time...too early and it can slow down cooking time, too late and it won't be properly absorbed into the food being seasoned.

When the Lord stated that Believers *are* salt, He pointed to a standard that we should all heed and follow. Like salt in the salt shaker, we are to be ready for action at all times. However, until we leave the shaker, we are only decorations gathering dust.

We must be sensitive to each situation into which we are "shaken." Too weak an application will leave a bland and unappealing taste...too heavy and it will be impossible to taste anything but the salt. As spiritual salt our mission is to lead others to experience the true flavor of life in Christ.

The Church was intended as a place for the collection and refinement of Believers. We must be prepared, though, to get out of the church pew...leave that Salt Shaker for Believers...and let the Lord apply us to someone who needs to be seasoned to His taste. Want to shake on it?

PARABLE OF THE WILLFUL WAY

There is hardly anyone around in this modern age who is not acquainted with a lady friend of mine. Well...she's not actually a friend. We haven't been properly introduced, after all. In fact, I don't even know her name. I've given her a nickname that I think suits her, though. I call her Ado Annie, after the character in "Oklahoma!" who can't say "No."

It's not what you think. Annie is the lovely female voice in my various GPS devices. You probably already have one or more of them yourself. It seems natural to give them a name, doesn't it?

I'll always remember my first experience with Annie. I bought the first device that was her residence from one of those on-line bargain sites for a really good price. I tried her out on some short local junkets, just so we could become accustomed to one another. We seemed to hit it off right away.

Then came the weekend I gave our relationship its first real trial...a three-hundred-mile trip to South Carolina. As you may know, there's nothing quite like being cooped up in an automobile for six hours straight to test the strength of a relationship. I learned a lot about Annie...and myself...during the course of that trek.

Everything started out fine...I discussed our point of origin and gave her the details about our destination. She carefully mapped out every step of the way, and told me that we'd be going the easiest way. She calculated the exact mileage...even knew how long it should take for us to arrive.

Our time together did not go completely without minor disagreements, however. In fact, even before we were out of our subdivision, we had our first little tiff. She suggested that I turn left instead of going straight at an intersection. I told her that I've been going straight at that point for twenty-five years or more and didn't see any reason to change. She didn't say "No," but simply informed me she was recalculating the route to accommodate my error.

There were one or two more incidents where I chose to go a more familiar way instead of yielding to her recommendations. She didn't disagree...just reminded me that it was necessary for her to recalculate the route to suit my whims. Her voice remained calm and pleasant, but it was clear that my stubbornness was an inconvenience...if not an annoyance...to her.

The long-distance portion of the trip went without incident, both on the way there and back. There was one period while we were in the foreign territory, however, that put quite a strain on our new relationship.

We were searching for the place where we were to meet friends for dinner. I got off on the wrong foot by missing a turn. Annie instructed, "Turn left in one quarter of a mile." I drove past the street before I saw it. She said, "Route calculation." Then she came back with, "Turn left at the next street," then "Turn left!" That didn't look as if it was going to get us where we wanted to go, so I didn't turn left. "Route calculation," she responded...I imagined that she sounded a little irked.

At the next intersection, Annie directed, "Turn left!" Same result. After several demonstrations of my willful determination to keep going, Annie's screen indicated that I should make a U-turn, as she intoned, "Turn around!" "Turn around!" at each available cross street.

It made me think of the episode on The Prairie Home Companion, when the hero continuously failed to follow the GPS voice's instructions. Finally, the voice blurted out, peevishly, "I don't know why you even turn me on...your never listen to me anyway!"

Well...we finally completed our trip and got back home all right. But that tense exchange with Annie started me thinking.

How many times during my Christian walk have I begun by relying on the Spirit's guidance, only to fail in following His clear indication of the way I should go? There have been countless times that He has suggested softly for me to "Turn left" or "Turn right," on those occasions when I have chosen to go a different way, according to some personal desire or whim.

In my experience, the urging of the Spirit is never impatient or annoyed by my behavior...completely without temper tantrums and accusations. No, the Spirit's message is a calm "Turn at the next opportunity," and, occasionally, "Turn around!" "Turn around!"

Much like my Ado Annie, the Spirit is persistent and longsuffering with us when we go on our willful way...quick to recalculate and adjust to allow for our failure to follow His directions...always offering an alternate route. Even as we hasten to our own destruction, He remains faithful to His promise to guide and direct us in the way we should go. It's up to us to follow...or not.

The only question in the matter of the Willful Way is this: Whose Will will prevail?

PARABLE OF THE TARDY TRAVELER

The Lunch Bunch got together the other day for our more-or-less monthly get-together at a local restaurant, and, as usual had a pleasant time of relaxed fellowship and good food. Our relationship goes back to high school in most cases and has survived all the usual tests, including early marriage, parenting, career developments, all manner of health and wealth changes...up to and through retirement and the increasing concerns of aging.

One of the recurring topics of conversation in recent years, since most of the group are retired, has been the sharing and comparing of travel experiences. As I have heard descriptions of numerous tours and cruises, I've thought about the many modes of transportation available today.

Have you ever stopped to think that it has only been in the last century of so that the vast majority of the world's population traveled more than a few dozen miles from the place where they were born? And those who ventured farther usually did so on foot, on horseback or by horse drawn conveyance over unpaved paths, trails and single-lane roads.

In less than three generations mankind has progressed from the horse and buggy to space crafts landing on the moon...from exploring continents to exploring solar systems and galaxies. All because of advances that have been made in the field of transportation.

Think about it...we have progressed from walking, to pulling or pushing carts and wagons, to putting rails under those carts and wagons. Then we devised motors to propel those carts and wagons, either on road or rail. Then some wizard learned how to lift those carts and wagons into the air and move them from place to place. The advent of better motors and engines...improved roads, rails and landing places...allowed us to move people farther and faster. What an age we live in!

But, have you noticed that, in spite of all these marvelous developments, travelers...from seasoned veterans to wandering neophytes...still have one complaint in common? The time it takes to get under way...delays, layovers, waits for baggage, or the limousine, or...whatever. And these days there are the time-consuming luggage checks and passenger pat-downs to check for anything that might be a threat to travelers' safety.

Less than one hundred years ago it took weeks to get from the United States to Europe. Today one can have breakfast at home and supper in Paris. And still, we fret over delays. The wise and wary traveler arrives at the airport or train terminal early...usually an hour or more ahead of time, just in case. Even with auto travel it's prudent to take into account the possibility of delays due to road work, accidents and rush hour traffic.

As I've written before, I tend to operate on the "just in time" principle...most of my life I have tended to allow twenty or twenty-five minutes for a twenty-minute trip. Although that works out well most of the time, sometimes it turns out badly.

It's true enough that when the pilot of an airliner, the driver of a bus or taxi, or the engineer of a passenger train is ready to depart, he isn't concerned whether a passenger has been waiting for hours or breathlessly ran to the gate at the last minute. Once that passenger is on board, he or she will be transported to the destination along with everyone else.

At a funeral service the other day, family and friends of the departed one gave testimony to the fact that he was a good man and friend, who lived an exemplary life. "Daddy wasn't a church-going man, but he was glad when Mom, my sisters and I became Christians." The only thing I could think of was, "I wonder if he got on board in time?"

I have heard of more than one person who, when responding to the testimony of a Christian, said something to the effect that, "I haven't lived a Christian life, and I'm not going to be a hypocrite and become one now, just because I'm in trouble." That's like saying that one didn't plan ahead to get to the airport on time, and it would be hypocritical to run the last hundred yards to get to the gate before they pull back from the gangway.

For all who have planned ahead and have lived a productive Christian life while awaiting your departure time, I say bon voyage. I'll see you in the Kingdom.

However, if you have chosen not to anticipate the journey...if you have gotten caught up in life's busy work and are in danger of becoming a tardy traveler...I urge you to get a move on. Don't risk being left at the station. And don't be embarrassed to run, if necessary, to get to the gate in time. The Pilot won't chide...the attendant angels won't criticize...nobody who matters will call you a hypocrite. In fact, we'll all rejoice to have you on board.

So...let me ask you: Do you have your ticket yet? If not, I can put you in touch with the Ticket Agent...and there are plenty of seats available, because there are always a lot of "no shows."

PARABLE OF THE WEEPING ONES

I talked many times with my dad about his conversion from one who was a good man who knew *about* God and Jesus and could quote the Bible, into a genuine Christian...one who *knew* God and Jesus and lived a Bible-based life. That experience came more than halfway through his seventy years of life.

Though baptized as a young pre-teen, and sent or taken to church on all the appropriate occasions, he said he came to a point where he realized he was a Christian by inclination only. He had never taken the step of asking the Lord to come into his life and take charge.

He told me he was shocked and humbled to discover that he had so little understanding of what it meant to *be* a Christian...to actually live daily, and relate to others, as a Christian.

He knew how to pray, he thought. He had recited many prayers that had all the right words and phrases...he had observed the proper posture for prayer...even used it on occasion. But when he attended his first prayer group meeting as a new convert, it dawned upon him that prayer was not a mere tip of the hat and nod of respect to God as you present Him with your list of wants and needs...that it was an actual conversation with God in expectation of His response.

He told me that it was at that moment of insight that he found himself next in the prayer circle...it was his turn to add a sentence prayer. He was overwhelmed, and in a panic, he uttered the only thing that came to his mind. "Jesus wept," he prayed. He vowed that night to never let that happen again. And that night he did become a prayer warrior.

Many young people, when challenged to learn a Scripture verse, latch onto that same text, John 11:35, "Jesus wept." It's the shortest verse in the King James Version of the Bible, of course. Because it is so short, it is easy to misunderstand why it's there, and what it really means.

Have you ever come across that verse and asked yourself "Why did Jesus' weep?" I have. Since my Dear One graduated into the Kingdom, I have learned something about that verse that brings it into focus for me. Let me share what the Spirit has showed me.

Was Jesus sad because His friend Lazarus had died? Or because He was too late to heal him? Or, perhaps, because Mary and Martha blamed Him for tarrying? Or even because the crowds were testing Him and didn't have faith that He could raise Lazarus? No, I don't think any of these things was the reason for His tears.

Think about it for a minute. Jesus had told the disciples earlier that He was present with the Father when the world was spoken into existence. He had walked the streets of eternity Himself...spent eons as one with the Father, and in the presence of His angelic worshipers... felt the unlimited freedom of the totally spiritual nature.

Our Lord had given up life in the Glorious Kingdom to become Perfect Man in order to foil the designs of the adversary and pay the penalty for our disobedience, so we could enjoy eternity there with the triune God of Creation.

He had BEEN there, my friend. And now, He knew that He must recall Lazarus from his newly claimed citizenship in that wonderful place, as evidence of His power even over death. He must return him to this sinful world, where he would experience the deaths of many of his loved ones, and, at some future date, the second death of his revived body.

I believe THAT'S why Jesus wept. It's as if He were saying, "I'm sorry to do this to you, my dear friend, but it's an important lesson that these people have to learn."

Our family has shed many tears...and shall no doubt shed many more...each time we think about the loss of our dear ones. After all, that's the way the Lord programmed us. But make no mistake about those tears, Beloved. We wouldn't bring them back from their new home in God's Kingdom even if it were within the power of those tears to do so.

Soon, when the scars of sadness are healed, we'll be able to look ahead with joy and the expectation of seeing and having fellowship with them again. And then there will be NO MORE PARTING, NO SORROW, NO SADNESS...and, especially, NO WEEPING.

So...weep with me, if you like...and I'll weep with you when you're overtaken by sorrow...but then let's devote ourselves to the business of leading others into the hope that is the promise to all believers...the certain hope of eternal life where there is only joy...and no more tears.

PARABLE OF THE UNCLAIMED BLESSING

Do you remember the child's card game called "Old Maid"? The cards are designed with pairs of matching pictures, plus one odd card with a picture of an unattractive woman bearing the title Old Maid. Of course, in this politically correct age I'm sure such a game has fallen from favor.

The term Old Maid originally referred to any woman above marriageable age...say, from eighteen to thirty-five, give or take a few years in either direction...who remained unmarried and childless. "Old" because she was considered to be outside the normal childbearing years, and "Maid" because she was still single.

According to that renowned fount of indisputable knowledge and information, Wikipedia, there are several other terms that are accepted as substitutes for the OM designation. One of the most common ones is "spinster," which apparently has been used since medieval times to refer to women who, because they had no husband to provide the family finances, resorted to spinning yarn, which was one of the few opportunities available to women for earning wages.

In addition to the term "spinster," Wikipedia also mentions the terms bachelorette, cat lady (after the image of a woman who prefers the companionship of her cat(s) to that of a husband) and Catherinette (a French term for single women above the age of twenty-five who are presumed to be under the protection of Sainte Catherine).

When I was growing up, although one might be referred to in private as an Old Maid, I was always told that was an impolite and disrespectful term. After all, that was the Golden Age of the euphemism, wasn't it? Instead, we politely spoke of Maiden Ladies and Unclaimed Blessings.

Is it better to call an otherwise eligible single female a Maiden Lady or Unclaimed Blessing than to label her an Old Maid? Hey! I have an idea. Why label her at all? Why not just call her by name without having her haul around that ball-and-chain tag?

You'll never guess what it was that brought about this observation of the honorable estate of un-marriage. It was, in fact, a news item about Unclaimed Blessings...just not the sort that I've been writing about so far.

The article made reference to an item covered on a morning TV show about the billions...yes, I said BILLIONS...of dollars of unclaimed money resting in the vaults and treasuries of every state in the Union. It said that a recent find in the Midwest netted a family over six million dollars, topping the previous record of over four million claimed by a family in New York.

Stocks were purchased years ago, but the certificates had been lost. Over the decades the value had grown immensely, resting in the state's treasury of unclaimed money, until discovered and claimed by the original owners' descendants. Talk about unclaimed blessings.

Financial advisors will tell you that there are several web sites that keep track of the unclaimed funds that are required by law to be retained by states, protected and held safely for the proper owners. It could be from sources as uncollected insurance payments, inactive bank accounts that have been closed by the banks, various types of refunds, etc.

I've been told that it is a good idea to check for these unclaimed funds sites in every state where one has resided and/or had business transactions. The same is true for one's relatives and family members. Whether direct or distant.

I'm convinced, however, that the greatest unclaimed blessing isn't a person, or any amount of property. Judging from the examples of many Believers, I think they are missing out on the grace, peace, comfort and joy that is available daily to each of us simply by placing our trust in Jesus. Six million...or six billion...dollars? That's nothing compared to what you have in Him. All you have to do is claim it.

PARABLE OF THE POWERFUL FLOWER

As the seasons change and the world around us takes on the appropriate costume for the time of year, have you ever noticed the kinds of things that your fellows praise and lament over? In Winter there are the crisp, clear air and the beauty of new-fallen snow...or the icy winds that cut like a knife and the hidden dangers of new-fallen snow.

The Summer offers opportunity for wonderful times outdoors and lovely, lush growth of gardens and lawns...or oppressive heat waves and the hot, hard work of keeping those gardens and lawns under control—and, of course, those dratted mosquitoes.

Fall brings relief from the heat and the expanding wonder of leaves changing from green monotone to a mind-numbing symphony of colors...or the chore of preparing for life indoors and the unavoidable labor of raking or blowing all those tons of lovely leaves.

Ah! but then there is Spring. I'm hard-pressed to think of something bad or unfavorable to say about Spring. (Well...OK, there *is* that thing about the pollen and allergies, but *besides* that. And, maybe, thunderstorms, tornadoes, the season's first sunburn...) The point is that almost everyone looks forward to Spring, and coming out of hibernation into the glorious light of days filled with the colors of buds and blossoms in outrageous array. Those flowers are like miniature vendors in nature's outdoor marketplace, waving to attract the attention of potential prospects for the prizes they offer.

If my yard is any measure, this must be the year of the Daffodil and the Jonquil. They seem to be growing *everywhere*, cropping up in unexpected places as if they had their own ideas of which parts of the lawn or woods needed additional ornamentation. And I must confess that I am hard-pressed to disagree with their judgment. They're like those pieces of bric-a-brac that make a home seem cozier.

As lovely as they are, however, there is much more to those blossoms than meets the eye. True, "a thing of beauty is a joy forever," but it is entirely as true that beauty without utility soon becomes tiresome and useless. After a few days, cut flowers droop, dry out and die...and, their decorative value gone, they're discarded.

After all, the flowering blossom of any plant is only one of Nature's marketing tools...specifically designed to attract "customers" in order to generate a net profit for the local branch of the species. Each flower advertises to birds, insects and, yes, people, that there is something of value to be found here.

As the insects browse among the blossoms, they oblige them by spreading their pollen from "shop to shop." They take away something of value to themselves and thereby profit the plants. The plants take that profit and turn it into seed-bearing fruit that matures in due time.

That fruit then becomes the next step in this clever advertising program by appealing to a new market: a whole new group of insects, birds, beasts and people, who select the fruit and take it away for their own satisfaction. These customers take away something of value...the plant gets what it wants, the spreading of its offspring. And the cycle goes on and on, season after season.

Wait a minute! Isn't all of life like that? We clean up, dress up and "smart up" in order to attract something that is of value to us, so that we can continue to survive and spread our kind. But it is only to the extent that we are willing to give up something that is of value to others that we can succeed. The truly successful person is one who has discovered what he or she has to offer that is valued by those around them, and promotes and provides it with persistence.

What is your Divinely designed and provided "flower"? Do others feel more valuable, more peaceful, more joyful, more confident, more powerful because of time they have spent with you? What will you *do* about that?

PARABLE OF THE NEW SONG

Among the many innovations credited to the internet generation is the addition of "YouTube" to our daily vocabulary. "I found this on YouTube," is one of the most common references cited these days...second only, perhaps, to Google. They're so common, in fact, that they are regularly "verbed"...you know...that's where a noun is used as a verb, as in "I Googled so-and-so," or "You should YouTube that."

Anyway...someone recently sent me a YouTube link to a talk given by Wintley Phipps, where he spoke about the pentatonic scale. He pointed out that most of the Negro spirituals were composed in the pentatonic scale...the five black keys on the piano...and said that in early America that was called the "slave scale."

Phipps then demonstrated by playing several spirituals on those black keys, climaxing with a stirring rendition of Amazing Grace. He suggested that John Newton, the man who wrote the first four verses of Amazing Grace, may have first heard the melody while he was the captain of a slave ship, bringing West African captives to the Americas. Google "Wintley Phipps" and "Amazing Grace" and you can see and hear it for yourself.

Several musicologists, not satisfied with the spiritual message and interpretation given by Mr. Phipps, sought to clarify and correct parts of his presentation. One added the information that the correct name was the "relative minor pentatonic scale," and consists of any series of notes 1, 3, 4, 5 and 7 using whole steps on the standard keyboard.

Another commentator wrote that the pentatonic scale can be played beginning on any note, black or white, on any instrument. He points out that in addition to a West African tradition, it has a tradition in Celtic folk music, Hungarian folk music, and the music of Greece and Southern Albania. It is also used in the tuning of the Ethiopian krar, Indonesian gamelan, Great Highland bagpipe, Philippine kulintang; and is the basis for melodies of Korea, Japan, China, India and Vietnam; not to mention the Afro-Caribbean and Polish highlander traditions.

Are you still with me? Hang on, we're almost there.

The thing that started me along this train of thought was a headline "New Song in Heaven: Going Beyond the Twelve-Tone Scale," an article by Mark Ellis, Senior Correspondent for ASSIST News Service. He was citing the frustration some composers feel as they attempt to avoid repetition in their music. He writes, "After 2,000 years, the limits of the 12-tone scale leave musicologists with a hunger for something more."

The part of the article that interested me concerned comments by Anne Ortlund, musician, popular Christian author and speaker. In her reference to the pentatonic scale that was used in ancient times by the earliest people groups and cultures, Ortlund suggests that the same five note arrangement may even "have preceded Babel, going back perhaps to the Garden of Eden."

She then points to an amazing development in the first century AD and notes, "When Christ came and the church was born, they stepped up to a 12-tone scale that no ears had ever heard before." Then she continues, "That's the way it will be in heaven. We will step up to something new - a new song - that we've never heard before, yet it will be based on something from the past."

I'll have to check the accuracy of her statement about the origin of the 12-tone scale sometime, but her point about the new song to be

sung by the Saints in the Kingdom is certainly according to Scripture. And I can testify to the awareness of a new song deep in my spirit since I learned to put my trust completely in the Master Musician.

I look forward to singing the new song in the Kingdom. But until the Conductor brings me in I'll be content to sing His praises here...whether in the pentatonic, the 12-tone or any other scale.

PARABLE OF THE SIMPLE QUESTION

 here is a familiar verse by Rudyard Kipling that has been a favorite of mine since I first read it. Perhaps you know it, too.

"I keep six honest serving-men
(They taught me all I knew);
Their names are What and Why and When
And How and Where and Who."

Kipling writes how these servants are kept busy, but are given a rest from time to time. Then he goes on to explain,
"But different folk have different views;
I know a person small—
She keeps ten million serving-men,
Who get no rest at all!"

Every parent and grand-parent...in fact, anyone dealing with children...understands exactly what Kipling is talking about. We've all have been faced with the seemingly endless barrage of questions about everything. And sometimes about nothing at all.

Whether one is a philosopher, teacher, theologian, or parent, it is important to understand that the most elemental building block of learning is the posing of a simple question. A familiar TV commercial puts it this way: "Inquiring minds want to know."

Much of the time the posing of a simple question is a legitimate attempt to gain knowledge...to expand understanding...to discover solutions to Life's problems. I don't think it is too far a reach to claim that all progress is based upon the thoughtful and persistent asking of the right questions.

It is also true, however, that questions can be used in a different way. Instead of being utilized as tools to discover and apply truths, questions can become offensive weapons, to accuse and express doubt and distrust. The devil is not called "the accuser" for nothing, you know.

In this year of political debate, the simple question is often used to distract voters from important issues and imply failings and misdeeds without actually having to accuse anyone. It's the old "Do you still beat your wife?" approach dressed in new clothing.

Almost every day someone can be heard to ask questions like "How could a loving God allow (you fill in the blank)?" Sometimes these simple questions are reasonable attempts to understand God's plan for us. Other times, however, the questions are put forward as evidence that God...if there is a God...could not possibly have the best interests of Mankind in Mind.

The Bible is full of questions about, and aimed at, God. Some are floated politely and gently, like bubbles rising into the heavens. Others, though, are more like howitzer shells, fired in anger and frustration by individuals facing dangerous and difficult times, or physical and emotional pain.

I like the prophet Habakkuk, who was an honest and sincere questioner of God. His simple questions were not selfish or for personal gain, but genuine, heartfelt inquiries into the nature of God, and His ultimate plan for His people and their enemies. We can know his questions were sincere because of the way God responded with answers.

We must never forget that God is not distracted or dismayed by our questions. His patience never fails...He always has the time to listen to our questions and complaints. It's also true, however, that His answers are often like those of any good parent, "Wait and see," "Not right now," and "No, that's not good for you."

Habakkuk asked questions like "God, don't you know?", "Why don't you listen?" and "When are you going to act?" God eventually answered that He did hear...that He had a plan for dealing with the problem...and that plan was already in motion. To me, the really marvelous revelation in this book is that Almighty God cares about... and even bothers to answer...our questions about His business here on earth.

In the end, Habakkuk's simple questions were answered, and he was satisfied. His final testimony in chapter 3:17-19 was that because he now understood God was indeed in control he wouldn't worry. Even if it seemed that everything was going wrong, he knew he could rejoice and trust in God.

God isn't intimidated, insulted or irritated by either your simplest or most complex questions. He cares for you and has only your best interests in His heart. Go ahead. Give Him your best shot. Then just sit back...relax...and pay attention as He provides the answer that will give peace to your mind and joy to your soul.

Any questions?

PARABLE OF THE GOOD GOSPEL

This is my writing morning, and I promised myself quite a while back that I would dedicate these designated times to writing down whatever the Spirit led me to develop into one of these inspirational Parables of mine. Sometimes I wake up with a topic already on my mind...other times I find the subject hidden on the list of Notes that I keep as a resource file...often the inspiration comes from a news item or an early-morning E-mail.

This morning I couldn't seem to focus on any of the usual sources, so I thought I would begin working on a list of music for our next presentation by the Singing Deacons, the Southern gospel quartet with which I sing. I had lined up the schedule for us to present a program at my church, so it was my turn to select the music to be used.

As I looked over a list of music we have sung and practiced over the last few years, and went through the index in a couple of hymnals I keep on hand, I was reminded of something. As is the case with just about any style of music one can mention, while Southern gospel music has a wide and enthusiastic fan base and can draw great crowds of the faithful to almost any concert, it also has a large body of people who don't care for it.

In my effort to understand the appeal...as well as the antipathy... accorded to gospel music I tried to analyze what its characteristics are, to define what factors make it unique. As I thought about it, I composed a quick haiku verse:

Simple, childlike faith;

Uncomplicated message.

That's Southern Gospel.

Interestingly enough, the same features of this style of music are pointed out by both sides as their reasons for loving or hating it. To some it's simple and straightforward...to others it's simplistic and naive. Whereas one group finds the words moving and inspirational, opponents are turned off by what they view as its sentimentalized and overly emotional expressions.

Fans of gospel music are stirred by its energy and excitement. Its detractors find it unsophisticated and unnecessarily showy. Some are attracted by the application of spiritual ideas to everyday problems and solutions; some are put off by its seeming lack of theological depth.

I've even heard devout Believers disagreeing over whether or not the music was well crafted...whether the words met the guidelines for good literature. Yes, among those familiar with Southern gospel music, there are seldom those who are entirely neutral concerning its value.

As I look back over the pros and cons of gospel music, there's one thought that comes to mind. Many of these same arguments can be applied to a discussion of almost any style of music.

Is there anyone in church anywhere who hasn't heard what we call Contemporary Christian music described as "7-11 music"— seven words repeated eleven times for emphasis? I don't believe that is intended as a recommendation or sign of approval. On the other hand, what about those who find traditional hymns and gospel music to be old fashioned and unexciting...who view hymns and anthems as "tedious and tasteless"?

Here's what I want you to take away from this discussion: whether the topic is music, or Christian denominations, or favored Bible translations or pet theological views...the fact is that there is hardly any variation that cannot appeal to a particular person's individual needs. As long as the focus and conclusion is the saving grace of God, offered to all who accept the sacrifice of blood for the forgiveness of personal sin, there is no such thing as "bad" gospel.

After all, "gospel" means "good news"...and there's no such thing as bad, good news. And that's the Gospel according to Jack. Amen?

PARABLE OF THE RESTORATION SPECIALIST

If I had known at the time how it would influence my life, I might have carved the time and date in stone...or had a plaque made...or, at least, jotted it down on a post-It note. Oh, that's right... we didn't have those sticky notes in the mid-sixties, did we? Well, anyway, I would have recorded the information some way for future reference.

It was during one of those conversations with my best friend from high school, Mac Willis, that he told me he thought I would like a book he had found very interesting, informative and extremely entertaining. It was called *The Furniture Doctor*, written by former advertising man George Grotz.

Grotz left a career on Madison Avenue— "too many geniuses," he said—and moved back to Vermont, where his family had lived for generations, and his "infamous Uncle George" had a refinishing shop. *The Furniture Doctor* was published in 1962, and there are now many improved, modern equivalents to some of the materials he recommends. However, I've found that the techniques he describes... and his basic philosophy that almost anyone can learn to handle the most common repair and refinishing tasks...still offer encouragement to the confirmed do-it-yourselfer.

In fact, it was largely on the basis of that encouragement that I eventually embarked on my late-life career of chair and rocker repair, refinishing and re-caning. It was chapters like "33 Ways to Restore Old Finishes," "Removin' Made Less Confusin'" and "Bleaching— The Blonds I Have Known," that gave me the idea that I really could master the craft of restoring antique chairs and rockers. Not that I've mastered it yet, but I've had a lot of fun in the process...and—if there's such a thing as a Hippocratic Oath for furniture repair—at least I have "done no harm."

I didn't start out intending to restore the chairs and rockers that I was asked to re-cane. It was simply that many of those brought to me for new seats were in such bad condition that they had to be fixed before they could be caned. So, armed with my trusty book, I took on the guise the restoration super-hero now known far and wide as Chairman.

Seriously, once I learned some of the restorer's secrets, I was willing to undertake furniture projects I never would have considered before. I have a collection of before and after photos that are evidence of many lessons, I learned from the pages of that one volume.

The right combination of chemicals, effort and patience, faithfully applied, can remove the most stubborn clear or opaque finish. And, in spite of what some would have us believe, the techniques for applying a new finish aren't nearly so mysterious that a layman can't master them. Sometimes repairs require woodworking equipment and skill, but many problems can be solved by the proper wielding of a rubber mallet, a screwdriver, some sandpaper and a little glue. Thank you, George Grotz.

This background from *The Furniture Doctor* has given me a new perspective on one of my favorite Scripture verses, Psalm 23. When the Psalmist sings, "He restoreth my soul," I now understand that he means so much more than "He makes my soul better."

When I restore a chair that is weathered, battered, mistreated and broken, I gently clean away the accumulated dirt and grime. Next, I strip away all remnants of the damaged finish, getting down to the bare wood. I apply a wash that removes stains and discolorations, and then a sealer and perhaps a stain to bring out the color and texture of the grain. A new finish covers and protects the wood, adding a luster and depth to its appearance. A properly applied finish enhances the natural beauty and helps it withstand the wear of everyday use.

When I read that the Shepherd restores my soul, it reminds me of the effort He takes to cleanse me and strip away those things that have marred my spiritual appearance. He fixes and tightens me up, making me fit for His use. But He doesn't stop there. He seals, finishes and polishes me, giving to my soul an inner beauty that is pleasing to Him.

And, following that restoration, He places me on display to be admired and used by others, just as He originally intended. Lest I take pride in my newly restored condition, it's important for me to recall that I'm no more responsible for my restoration than those chairs and rockers that I have worked on. All the praise and glory belong to the one and only Restoration Specialist.

PARABLE OF THE TROUBLE SWAP

There's an old story about a village where the people were constantly grumbling and complaining. No one was happy or satisfied. Envy, bickering and disagreement were everywhere. Every person seemed to be preoccupied with his or her own trials and troubles...all were discontented with their lot in life.

The pastor of one of the local churches became impatient with all the dissatisfaction and strife among his parishioners and proposed a solution. "Each of you bundle up your troubles and bring them to the church next Sunday, and we'll have a swap meet. That way you can get rid of your own troubles and at the same time you can help someone get rid of theirs...a double blessing."

The following Sunday the church parking lot was filled with members bringing in their troubles. Some carried small parcels, while others staggered under heavy burdens. Soon all the troubles were spread out...the members wound their way around the area, sorting through the stacks and piles...testing and trying on items they found appealing.

At the end of the day, each member gathered up their choices and triumphantly carried them back home...bearing home exactly the same troubles with which they had come, finally satisfied that things weren't nearly as bad as they thought...compared to the troubles of their fellows.

Perhaps that story was the basis of the parody on the old gospel hymn, "Leave It There." The parody ends with, "Take your burden to the Lord...then bring it home."

I've asked myself many times why there is so much unhappiness and dissatisfaction around us all day, every day. The news has been filled recently with reports of people railing out against the "evil, greedy rich" and wanting them to share more of their wealth with the "less fortunate." I haven't seen any such demonstrations against the "evil, greedy poor"...you know, the ones who steal, mug, car-jack and murder to get what they want, instead of working honestly for it. Have you?

The sad fact is that it is a trait of human nature to focus more completely on the possessions and abilities of others and value them more highly than we do our own. Our own burdens seem greater, when compared to the advantages and opportunities of others. We think, "How is that fair?"

Although the story of the Trouble Swap is merely a fable, the moral is still accurate. I daresay that, given the opportunity to properly investigate and understand the burdens born by those we tend to envy, we would probably prefer our own. "Better the devil we know," as the saying goes.

There is a simple truth, however, with which many, if not most, people fail to come to grips. It's an open secret...well known to all Believers: For all who accept the truths of the Bible, there is a promise that deals finally with all this concern about troubles and burdens...a promise which makes it, as one of my friends used to say, a "mute" point...one that has been forever resolved.

Jesus promised, "Come unto me, all you who are weak and heavy laden, and I will give you rest." He tells us His yoke is easy and His burden is light.

Do you understand the message of the yoke? Have you ever seen one? More importantly, have you ever seen a yoke for *one*? Every yoke I've ever seen was for two animals, whether oxen or some other beasts of burden.

So, then, what Jesus promises is this: When we bring our burdens and troubles to Him, He doesn't say He'll take them away or swap them, but, more importantly, that He'll stand in the yoke *with* us, sharing the weight and helping to bear the load. Technically we aren't to take our burdens to the Lord and leave them there, but to allow Him to join with us in successfully dealing with them and carrying them to a satisfying and blessed conclusion...in fellowship with Him.

I'd say that's better than any Trouble Swap we could ever devise, wouldn't you?

PARABLE OF THE POWER OF WORDS

Have you ever noticed that there are certain words that have the power to take charge of our thoughts and influence our actions and attitudes? Some of them are sentimental, and we keep them to ourselves, sometimes, out of embarrassment.

Love is one of those words. Loving others requires a level of tenderness and surrender that can make one vulnerable; a lowering of the barricade that protects the heart from attack. Love is seldom fatal, although it has great potential for pain and disappointment, which never goes away. And, Love sometimes leads the one who is overwhelmed by it to make sacrifices that are greater than life. For the most part, however, Love is a condition which is manageable over extended periods of time…even a lifetime.

Some words are capable of producing strong emotions, and leading to impressive outbursts of action, either offensive or defensive in nature. Hate is such a word. You don't often hear that word spoken calmly, in polite, conversational tones. Usually there is tension in the voice that expresses it, and a look of disapproval, perhaps of accusation—and that is true whether the one speaking it is on the attack or seeking protection behind it. The trouble with Hate is that often it leads one—on whichever side of the word one may be—to say and do hateful, mean and spiteful things. Things which affect not only the targeted individual, but countless uninvolved bystanders. Hate is highly contagious and can prove fatal. But it has a sure and certain remedy: Love.

Some words are so threatening that they fill our hearts with dread and bring us to the brink of despair. They are so frightening, in fact, that we replace them with all sorts of euphemisms—as if by renaming them we can take away some of their threat, reduce their power over us.

The first one of those words is...Cancer. How many of us have heard...you know, the "C" word...pronounced over ourselves, or a loved one, and felt a little part somewhere deep inside us begin to wither in a drought of doubt and uncertainty? How many people have heard that awful word, cashed in their chips, packed their mental suitcases and gone down to the dock to wait without hope for that dreaded boat to take them to the other side? But even Cancer is not always deadly.

Another word capable of stirring up strong emotions is a religious one: Sin. Now, don't tune me out yet, please, because, whether you believe it or not, the Biblical concept of Sin explains some of the most perplexing problems affecting our society...and, in fact, our world... today. It does require, however, the allowance for the possibility of a Divine authority—let's use the word: God—Who exercises power over the Universe. With that one concession, Sin can be defined in non-theological terms as "anything one says, does or thinks that one knows God doesn't like." The Bible says the penalty for Sin is death. Sin has no degree, large or small. And Sin has no effective cure—it is *always* fatal. There is, however, an antidote that transfers the effect of Sin from the sinner.

That brings us to another of those words that exercise such power over us that it has the ability to rob us of all joy. Most folks don't like to talk about Death. We talk about someone being deceased, lifeless, or, before the fact, terminal. We say they have "gone to the other side," "crossed the river Jordan," or sometimes they've simply "passed." If we are in a group of friends from church, we might say a loved one has "gone to be with the Lord," "left us for a better place," and maybe just "gone home."

The word Death is so final, colorless, leaving no room for hope. As the old-timer said, "Son, there aren't none of us goin' to get out of this alive." However, though there is no cure for Death, God offers a treatment that eliminates its finality.

The thing that brought this all to my mind, was a phrase I heard on the news the other day. The newsman said, while reporting on the health of a prominent figure, "The condition is not curable, but it is treatable." That phrase found a resonance in my heart, because I had heard it spoken in a doctor's office recently. "It's Stage Four," he said. "Out of ...?" I asked. "Four," was the reply.

The loud scuffling, I heard in my head was Hope, Joy, Assurance, Peace, Happiness…all striving to get out the door at once. But it was held firmly shut by the Dear One on the other side, who is able to keep my heart and mind fixed on Him. Once the shock diminished, all those Gifts of the Spirit are back under His control, and actively working to produce fruits to glorify Him.

There's a lot more to Life than merely living…and a lot more to Death than merely dying. If we concentrate on living in Love and dying with faith in the One Who paid the penalty for our sin with His own death, then death is far from the most fearsome and terrible thing that can happen to us on this earth.

Love, Hate, Sin, Death…even Cancer…are just words, now. Words that no longer have the power to remove or diminish the joy that comes from belonging to Him. It is the responsibility of each one who has experienced that joy to spread the message to everyone with whom we come in contact, that "Life is a condition that is not curable, but it is treatable," and "Death is not the worst thing that can happen to one who loves Jesus and trusts Him to save."

PARABLE OF THE LAUGHING PLACE

It's such an old joke that I hesitate to repeat it...but I will anyway. In the early days of the Old West, a rider galloped into the fort, slumping in the saddle, his body riddled with arrows. One of the soldiers asked, "Are you all right, cowboy?" "Yup," he groaned, "It only hurts when I laugh."

I've written any number of times about what I think of as Laugh Therapy. Although I've never heard of anyone else using the phrase, I'm probably not the first one to express the thought regarding a physical, emotional or psychological condition, that "It only hurts when I *don't* laugh."

When I was a young person, one of my favorite movies was Walt Disney's "Song of the South." Its story centers around several tales by Joel Chandler Harris, as related by his character, Uncle Remus.

Before you say anything, I know...the movie and the stories themselves have fallen from favor because they romanticize the disgraceful practice of slavery. However, that doesn't take anything away from the entertainment value, or the wisdom and philosophical value of the Uncle Remus stories, any more than it detracts from those of another famous slave, Aesop, of fable fame.

In the movie, Uncle Remus recounts the tale of Br'er Rabbit and the Laughing Place, whereby the wily rabbit escapes the clutches of Br'er Fox and Br'er Bear by leading them to his secret laughing place, which turns out to be a thicket containing a hornets' nest. In their haste to outrun the hornets, they forget the rabbit, shouting "I thought you said it was a laughin' place!" He calls after them, "I said it was *my* laughin' place, Br'er Fox, and I sho' is laughin'."

In typical Disney fashion, there's a song sequence where Br'er Rabbit sings "Everybody's got a laughin' place, a laughin' place to go-ho-ho. Take a frown, turn it upside down, and you'll find yours I know-ho-ho." You can look it up for yourself, if you know how to Google or Yahoo. Check it out on You Tube, like I did the other day.

Another of my favorite movies is "Singing in the Rain." And, as you might guess, one of the sequences I like best in that movie is where Donald O'Connor performs "Make 'Em Laugh." Classic. You can find that on You Tube, too.

Laughter has a multitude of benefits. Singers and speakers use prolonged laughter to improve breath control. Physical therapists use belly laughs as one way to strengthen the body's "core." Physicians have found that laughter can provide mild cardio-vascular exercise and relieve stress.

I've found all those things to be true for me. Those aren't the main reasons I recommend regular hearty laughter, though.

In Proverbs15:13, we read, "A merry heart makes a cheerful countenance, but by sorrow of the heart the spirit is broken." Those laugh lines on the face are one sign of a strong, healthy spirit.

Verse 15 says, "All the days of the afflicted are evil, but he who is of a merry heart has a continual feast." Whenever we are tempted to focus attention on mishaps and misfortunes, and on the misbehavior of others it's difficult to be optimistic. However, the ability to see humor in a situation provides nourishment for the soul.

One last Proverb on the subject is found in chapter 17, verse 22. "A merry heart does good like a medicine, but a broken spirit dries the bones." There is plenty of documented evidence that "Laughter is the best medicine."

In several of his books, the author Frank Peretti personifies the minions of the adversary...those demons, imps and other evil beings... and makes them visible to the reader. He portrays them performing physical acts of harassment and torment upon the characters of his stories. Although some deny the theological soundness of these portrayals, I find them helpful in finding a means to defend myself from the methods and stratagems of the adversary.

Whenever I encounter what one of my friends used to call "clods in the churn of life," I imagine one of those evil ones standing nearby, thinking he has caused me to suffer a spiritual setback. That's when I take a second or two to just laugh at him and his feeble efforts. I can't help but believe that takes some of the fun out of his misbehavior... and that makes me laugh more.

So...that's my laughing place. That's the place where I can always count on a few moments of freedom from the broken spirit, the evil and the spiritual drought that afflict so many, robbing them of the joy that rightfully belongs to all Believers.

Have you found your laughing place yet? Remember, my friend, it really only hurts when you *don't* laugh.

PARABLE OF THE WIDE RECEIVER

I don't know where you are as you read this, but as I write it is nearing the end of the football season. At least to the extent that teams are now preparing for the year's Bowl games and NFL playoffs. I know, I know...by the time the Super Bowl is done we'll be half-way through Winter. But anyway, for most of us who are casual sports fans, it's near the end of the season.

I grew up in a family where—at least for the men—football was arguably the main reason for getting the family together at Thanksgiving, Christmas and New Year's Day. Since our girls have grown and married, however, that tradition has dwindled to a minor element in our gatherings. Not necessarily a bad thing, since the guys don't spend the days hunkered in front of the TV, munching snacks, slapping each other on the back and making guttural howls and moans as the images on the electronic cave wall flash to and fro.

In the sports segment of the evening news recently there was what I would say was definitely the catch of the day. The receiver was streaking down the sidelines, the defender matching him stride for stride. The pass was aimed perfectly, leading him by just enough so that he had to stretch flat out to make the catch. The ball reached his hands just as they broke the plane of the goal line, and the wide receiver held it tightly as he did a jarring belly-flop in the end zone.

That wide receiver's performance made an impression on me for another reason as well. Our young pastor's sermon text that day was John 1:1-13. When he read verse 12, one of those divine spotlights focused on the word "received." And, as so often happens, while he preached on, the spirit began to speak. "...As many as *received* Him, to them gave he the power to become the children of God, even to them that believe on his name."

In football the wide receiver runs down the field hoping the ball will be thrown to him, and intending to *do* something with it...run toward the goal. Are there "receivers" in other sports? I can't think of one. In baseball the catcher stops the ball, but most of the time his job is just to return it to the pitcher. In hockey or soccer, the goalie blocks the puck or the ball, but isn't expected to do much with it. OK, I suppose catching a tossed or kicked ball or puck could technically be called receiving, but to my mind that's not quite the same.

What does it mean to receive something, after all? There are a lot of wide receivers who never get their hands on the ball. Some of those who do never get the chance to go anywhere with it. What does it really imply when it says they "received" Him?

Back to the pastor's sermon for a minute. His son "received" a birthday gift—a new game he had wanted. When his grandmother offered to play it with him, he protested, "I can't! It says it is for Ages 7 and up, and I won't be seven until tomorrow."

Perhaps he understood something that we adults have missed. He had *accepted* the gift, but couldn't actually *receive* the gift until he could put it to use. In the same way, many knew Jesus...accepted Him as a man...but did nothing about the fact.

It isn't enough to merely *accept* the fact of Jesus's claim as the Son of God. Our success as believers depends upon how we *receive* Him after we grasp His Truth. After all, a successful reception requires us to do something. Let us receive Him, face toward the goal, then "run with patience the race that is set before us." Amen?

PARABLE OF THE RESPONSIBLE ONE

It was 1960 when Broadway first shined stage lights on the show "Bye Bye, Birdie." It was a musical based roughly on the big story in the news reports of the day concerning the drafting of popular rock star Elvis Presley into the Army. It was made into a movie in 1963, and has been produced in countless road shows and high schools around the country ever since.

Birdie was the source of several hit songs. Probably the best known are "Put on a Happy Face," "A Lot of Living to Do," and "Kids." Of them all, though, it's "Kids" that came to mind the other day. Check out the lyrics and see if you can guess why.

Kids! I don't know what's wrong with these kids today!

Kids! Who can understand anything they say?

Kids! They're disobedient, disrespectful oafs!

Noisy, crazy, dirty, lazy, loafers!

While we're on the subject:

Kids! You can talk and talk till your face is blue!

Kids! But they still just do what they want to do!

Why can't they be like we were,

Perfect in every way?

What's the matter with kids today?

I'm not sure exactly what I was doing, but the TV was on, its sound floating around on the perimeter of my consciousness, when the talking...sometimes shouting...heads began to discuss, in the words of the song, "What's the matter with kids today?" And, more particularly, whose fault it is that they are turning out the way they are.

Their casual view toward sex and marriage...their preoccupation with material things...their lack of interest in basic rules of etiquette... their increasing cynicism towards the standards and practices of a society from which they feel alienated...(feel free to insert your own pet peeve about their behavior here). Who or what is responsible for what many view as the increasing purposelessness of this new generation of young people?

Whose fault, is it? Parents? Media? Peer pressure? Is it the result of the Age of the Instant...with Text Messaging, YouTube, Facebook and Twitter...whereby they can access more information than any previous generation and share it faster and more completely, whether or not they understand its significance?

Who's to blame? Who is responsible for this mess?

I believe that one of our problems today is that we feel such a need to define the cause of bad conduct and assign the blame where it doesn't belong. I've written before about our tendency to child-proof the world instead of world-proofing the child. Instead of teaching and encouraging safe practices, we require helmets and knee pads. Instead of insisting on high moral values and thoughtful behavior, we recommend "safe sex" and social bubble wrap. Who's to blame, indeed.

Miss Dew was one of the finest Math teachers I ever knew. She taught me Trigonometry, gave me every rule and technique known to science for effective solution of any type of Trig problem I could imagine. Was it her fault that I got a D in her class? The lowest Math grade in my whole school career? Of course, she was certainly not responsible for my failure to properly follow and apply the principles she so carefully and meticulously taught.

If we apply the current wisdom, we could imply that if Miss Dew had only understood me better...had taken a more personal interest in my needs and wants...spent more "face time" with me I could have made at least a B...maybe even an A. It wasn't really my fault, was it?

Of course, it was.

No matter how often we claim temporary insanity, multiple personality disorder, or bipolar disorder...as real as those may be in some situations...there is one unescapable fact we all must eventually face: There comes a time when we each must take responsibility for our own actions and misdeeds. As my grandmother used to say, "Every pot has to sit on its own bottom."

My own ideas of what is right and wrong...my social, moral and ethical values...come from what I have studied and accepted from the Bible. The Bible tells us without exception or qualification that although we are "fearfully and wonderfully made," "there is none righteous, no, not one."

One recent news report quoted one of the weakest excuses for misdeeds I've ever heard: "Errors were made" the person intoned...as if to imply "It's not really my fault, but even if it was, I really didn't mean it." Face it, folks, the ultimate responsibility must eventually fall upon the one who committed the error. "The devil made me do it!" makes good comedy, but it won't work here.

There was a popular restaurant in Atlanta years ago with a sign over the coat rack that read "Please keep an eye on your own coat. The management is irresponsible."

In that day when our works are tried in holy fire, we will not be judged based upon what some irresponsible person did to influence our actions, but on our actions themselves and the secret intentions of our heart at the time. Good or bad...we *will* be held responsible.

PARABLE OF THE PRICELESS POSSESSIONS

Every home has one. Or, more accurately, every *person* has at least one, if I am any example. They go by many names, depending upon the personality and temperament of their owners. Whether known as a place for keepsakes, unsorted treasures and knick-knacks or as permanent/temporary holding cells for countless miscellaneous items in suspension until one takes the time to put them where they really belong. In the latter case, the usual designation is "The Junk Drawer."

I've written before (i.e., Parable of The Brick) about my propensity to hold on to anything...anything at all...that might be of use sometime in the indeterminate future. If the object in question is pocket-size or smaller, it is likely to end up in the Junk Drawer. In Southern terms, I suppose I could call it my "fixin' to" drawer—as in, "I'm fixin' to put this (fill in the blank) where it belongs."

Now, there are two ways to define the word "priceless." The most common usage is in the sense of having a value...whether sentimental or otherwise...that is beyond price. A work of art may be thought of as so rare that a monetary valuation is meaningless. That angelic expression on the face of a much-loved grandchild is something that money can't buy. It's priceless.

On the other hand, there is the sense in which an item has no apparent value...no obvious use, at least at the present time...perhaps no discernable future use, either. These are the bits of the daily debris of life that end up in one's pockets at night and seem too good to be thrown into the trash.

My dear Lyn had for many years a small box in which she kept her personal treasures. She had an accumulation of things that were *price*less to her...pr; *less* to anyone else. Many of the items I could identify from our pre- and post-courting days. Things like ticket stubs, programs and imprinted napkins from social events...even one or two numbered "car hop cards" from the Varsity Drive-in in Atlanta (Not old enough to know what those were? Ask me or any old-time Atlantan about them sometime.). It would have been pointless to suggest that any of those memorabilia could or should be thrown away. Their value to her was without measure...priceless.

In the same way, the very thinking that caused things to be placed in the keepsake/junk drawer in the first place resists the urge to dispose of them at some later time. So the clutter continues to gather, until it threatens to overwhelm us.

The good news is that I occasionally find a useful application for something in one of my junk drawers...after thirty years in the dark of that place, an object proves to be just the thing I need for some project that's at hand. The bad news is evident when I realize I recently disposed of what would have been just the thing for some other project.

It came to me the other day that human memory is a lot like one's keepsake/junk drawer. I believe *that's* where life's priceless possessions reside, not in houses, bank accounts, cars and investments. Things are subject to fire, wind, flood and theft. Memories are ours forever.

In all fairness, however, I have to admit that there are any number of memories and recollections in my consciousness which I don't want there any longer...they make up what I think of as the junk that I would like to sort out and dispose of. They seem only to serve as distractions from the peace and joy which are rightfully mine as a Believer.

I recall Garrison Keillor saying, "When you're a writer, there's no such thing as a bad experience. Everything is material." Perhaps he's right. Perhaps all the bits and pieces tossed into the junk drawer that is our memory have served to make us...and serve to remind us...who we are, and from whence we've come. Sometimes the junk helps keep the priceless things in perspective.

God equipped each of us with a mental keepsake/junk drawer. Go to yours often. That's the place for your priceless possessions until they're transferred to your storehouse in the Kingdom.

PARABLE OF THE
GOOD WORD

I had a topic in mind to write about this morning...one that had nudged its way into my mind a few mornings ago during my necessary walk with Miss Suzy. The idea was waiting patiently in the "green room" of my mind, like a guest celebrity on a TV talk show, ready for its interview.

Before I called it onstage, however, I made a rookie mistake...one that no experienced producer would have made. As I settled down to begin, I took a quick look at the day's top news items to be sure the earth was still in its proper orbit. That's when I became distracted by one of the articles, which elbowed its way past the intended feature and barged onto my mind's set.

"How rude!" I thought. However, with true Southern gentility, the original thought agreed to return at another time so that the newcomer could be thoroughly explored.

"I'll get back to you later to hear your story," I whispered softly as I escorted the idea back to the green room and returned my attention to the newcomer. (I know it probably sounds silly, but sometimes I imagine that's how things take place within the confines of my mind.)

Anyway...the news story that ended up in the guest chair today is one that has been talked about in the field of Information Technology—read that "computer stuff"—and one that should be of interest to anyone who uses any form of computer or smart phone. The subject was how to make passwords more secure and easier to remember.

As a word-smith and sometime writer I receive considerable joy and satisfaction in devising clever and creative passwords for bank accounts, credit cards, online accounts...in short, any place an information mugger might try to steal my name, money or property. According to this article by Taylor Hatmaker, I can definitely do a lot better at protecting myself. So can you, I suspect.

A 2009 investigation into a computer hacking scandal found that the most popular password in use was "123456". The second and third most common passwords were also strings of consecutive numbers. And, in a clever display of genius and creativity, the fourth most common password was...wait for it... "Password."

To avoid passwords that would be simple to hack, the writer cautioned against using any information about yourself that might be easily obtained from public knowledge, such as name, E-mail or street address, birthday, etc. It was also pointed out that consecutive numbers and any combination of words and terms in the dictionary can be hacked by any good cracking program.

Some of the tips to increase password safety include:

1. Use a combination of upper- and lower-case letters, numbers and symbols. Twenty-six letters, each in upper and lower case...ten numbers...1500 symbols...arranged in what to an intruder and his program appear to be random order, make it many times more difficult to break into your personal material.

2. Use the maximum length allowed for your password. Do that by padding a simple password with symbols that you can remember. In the example cited in the article, an automated hacking program cracked the password "mOOse44" in less than a second. On the other hand, alter the password to mOOse44! and, "Assuming that the hacking software is guessing one hundred billion combinations a second, believe it or not, it could take the same software almost 200,000 centuries to crack it."

Here's the conclusion I've reached as a result of this simple news item: Most of us spend a lifetime working to amass and protect things... and people, too, for that matter...only to discover that our best efforts can be easily thwarted by the adversary and his evil band of happiness hackers. Their hacking techniques utilize all of the assorted setbacks, calamities and disasters of life that can come upon us unexpectedly. We are so vulnerable to his well-practiced methods and strategies, aren't we?

When you feel helpless and in despair in the face of these threats to your spiritual security, I can tell you upon good authority that there is a single password that can protect you from the most vicious onslaught. You can invoke it at any time...as often as you wish... without penalty or price.

On top of everything else, this password is easy to remember; it isn't case sensitive...no need to worry about upper or lower case; and it doesn't require numbers, symbols or padding to be effective. The password...the Good Word that will protect you now and through eternity...is "Jesus."

Since Jesus became my password, my identity has been secure, and everything I value in life has been kept out of the reach of all who would try to rob them from me...kept "safe and secure from all alarms," as the old hymn promises to those leaning on the everlasting... password.

What's *your* Good Word?

PARABLE OF THE DEFINITE DEADLINE

I had heard the story before, but just be sure, I went to the top of Mount Google to inquire of the all-knowing oracle concerning the origin of the expression "meet a deadline." Yes, my memory had served me well...Google confirmed my understanding.

Google said, as I had heard many years ago, that the first use of the expression dated back to the Civil War. Although most authorities agree that it was first used by the Confederate officer who was in charge of the prison at Andersonville, Georgia, there is some opinion that it was in more or less general use among prisons on both the Union and the Confederate sides.

The stockade at Andersonville was made up of timbers 15 feet high, buried about 5 feet in the ground. About twenty feet inside of that stockade was a line marked by narrow planks atop stakes that were driven into the ground. Prisoners were warned that anyone venturing beyond that delineated line were to be shot. That line was called the "dead line." There were also reports of at least one Union prison, located in Rock Island, Illinois, with a similar dead line.

Since those early origins, of course, the word deadline indicates a final opportunity to take an action or make a decision. Each of us deals with the challenge of deadlines almost every day. If we fail to respond by that deadline, the offer is withdrawn, the opportunity is lost.

The idea of crossing over a deadline came to mind a few days ago when we waved goodbye to a friend we had put on a bus to another city. We were sure to get her to the station almost an hour ahead of the scheduled departure time to insure she would get a good seat. As a consequence, she was second in line when time came to board the bus.

We watched as the traffic light turned green and the bus moved off toward its destination. As it began to move away, we heard a soul-wrenching scream from behind us.

"BUS!! STOP! STOP! PLEASE STOP!" cried a breathless young woman as she ran after it. She continued to weep as she got out her cell phone to call for help. She had missed the deadline. The bus had pulled away from the station, and the person who had brought her had also gone.

Whether her plight was the product of poor planning, unforeseen traffic delays, or what my dad used to call "a causal relationship with time," the result was the same. She missed the bus and was left behind.

I don't know a single person who doesn't have to struggle with schedules every day. Whether with social commitments, business obligations, or something as mundane as meeting the school bus or getting to a doctor's appointment...almost everyone I know finds it necessary to struggle with juggling each day's responsibilities to get everything done by some real or imagined deadline.

One philosopher observed, "Life is what happens while we rush to take care of something urgent." In other words, we often are so pressed to deal with some presumed urgent matter that we rush past some of the most important things in life. All because of the idea that we must meet some deadline or other.

Yes, deadlines and missed opportunities are a fact of life, aren't they?

However, each time I think of that young woman, in distress because she had missed her bus, there is another picture that comes to mind. Whereas she had missed the bus she had hoped to ride, there would be another one leaving for the same destination later that day. She would have another chance to get where she wanted to go.

God's Word reminds us in stern warning, "It is appointed unto men once to die..." (Hebrews 9:27, KJV) I suppose you could say that's the ultimate deadline, couldn't you?

It might seem strange to a casual reader of the Bible that the Spirit should lead the writer to insert that warning in the middle of a discourse about the process and the purpose of the sacrifice of God's Son on behalf of the world. I believe, however, that it fits in perfectly with the thought of deadlines and missed opportunities.

Each of us will face the ultimate deadline. Whether strolling casually or running at full speed, we will all approach our personal deadline, as it is appointed. What then? The verse in Hebrews continues, "...but after this the judgment." There will be a point where we will learn whether we have arrived—have made the proper decisions—in time to meet God's deadline for each of us.

There will be countless masses of those who have neglected to accept the offer of salvation from their personal sin, only to discover too late that the salvation bus has left them behind. No matter how loudly they cry, or how earnest their intentions at the last minute, without accepting the payment Jesus has made for their sins, they will be left at the station, awaiting their judgment.

The chorus of the traditional spiritual "Mary Had a Baby," observes sadly, "The people keep a-Comin' and the train's done gone." As you observe those around you, can you imagine how they will react as they approach their own individual deadlines? Will it be with confidence, or will it be with a panicked cry for the bus to stop?

What about yourself? Do you have assurance that your reservation has been made in time? That your seat on the Heavenly

bus is secure? If so, you can look forward to the ride. If not, I have a personal relationship with the divine Ticket Agent, Jesus Christ, and I can put you in touch with Him so you'll never again dread the definite deadline.

INDEX